"**A must-read for C(**
Account Management te
accelerate grow................**omer base."**

Ashvin Vaidyanathan, VP of Customer Success at LinkedIn
and Author of *The Customer Success Professional's Handbook*

REACH

A FRAMEWORK FOR DRIVING REVENUE GROWTH FROM YOUR EXISTING CUSTOMERS

ROD CHERKAS

The Best-Selling Author of
The Chief Customer Officer Playbook

Copyright © 2024, Rod Cherkas.
All rights reserved.

No part of this book may be reproduced or transmitted in any form or by any means, electronic or mechanical, including photocopying, recording, or by any information retrieval system, without permission in writing from the publisher.

Publishing Process by Weston Lyon
www.PlugAndPlayPublishing.com

Book Cover by Dave Praetorius
www.LisaLarter.com

Graphics by Sharon Holmes and
Tracey Miller | design@traceofstyle.com

Developmental Editing by Dan Janal
Line Editing by Jenny Butterfield Lyon

ISBN: 9798320139371

Disclaimer: This book contains opinions, ideas, experiences, and exercises. The purchaser and/or reader of these materials assumes all responsibility for the use of this information. Rod Cherkas and Publisher assume no responsibility and/or liability whatsoever for any purchaser and/or reader of these materials.

To my family, for their unwavering support and inspiration, and to the customer-facing professionals who recognize that every interaction is an opportunity to reach new heights.

What Others Are Saying About *REACH*

"If we launch this framework where I could train my teams to be great at identifying expansion opportunities and how my teams should be walking customers through the pipeline, that would be gold for me, absolute gold."

—**Maranda Dziekonski,** SVP of Customer Success at Datasembly

"*REACH* hits the exact focus that my Board of Directors and CEO are asking me about - accelerating revenue growth from our customer base. Rod's excellent framework helps us capitalize on the huge TAM potential sitting with a large number of our accounts."

— **Tony Smart,** Chief Customer Officer at Whip Around

"Customer Success has been missing a methodology that delivers predictability for identifying and delivering growth opportunities in our customer base. With *REACH*, Rod provides a structure that is easy to understand and implement and fills this key gap."

— **Rob Schmeltzer,** VP of Customer Success at Risk Optics

"*REACH* is a must read for any Customer Success Leader who wants to move the perception of his or her team from being seen as a cost center to a solid contributor to the company's revenue. *REACH* is a simple and easy-to-follow framework that will leave its mark on your organization."

— **Jonathan Schradi,** Senior Director of Global Customer Success at Scandit

"The ability of our CSMs to generate expansion is very personality-driven. We have some people who are excellent at it and tend to be very systematic in what they do. However, even the people who are excellent at generating expansion income lack a structured approach. Rod's framework adds that rigor for the whole team."

— **Nathan Jones,** VP of Customer Operations at Synack

"*REACH* provides metrics-driven insight into how the account is doing and its growth potential. That helps us focus on which accounts we should be paying attention to and which ones we shouldn't bother with."

— **Carly Bell,** Head of Customer Success at VergeSense

"I wish someone had written this book for Customer Success years ago."

— **Laura Lakhwara,** former Director of Customer Success at UiPath

"The REACH Framework™ really resonates. It empowers our teams to proactively uncover growth opportunities and apply a structured process to help customers realize the full value of our solutions. Rod's approach helps us decide where to invest our efforts."

— **Tracy Henriques,** VP of Customer Success at Salsify

"There's a million of these sales-training systems for generating the first sale, but there's nothing like those systems for expanding an account after that initial sale. That's what Rod has designed."

— **Robbie Baxter,** Founder of Peninsula Strategies and author of *The Membership Economy*

"Most enablement trainers try and squeeze Customer Success into a version of whatever methodology is for sales. But those people aren't salespeople. What our Customer Success teams are doing is too important to not have a consistent process like Rod's REACH Framework™."

— **Roderick Jefferson,** VP of GTM Enablement at Siteimprove and author of *Sales Enablement 3.0*

"*REACH* is an accessible and immediately actionable read. This is a very relevant book with real-world anecdotes sprinkled throughout and a clear framework to scorecard opportunities."

— **Jeremy Myers,** VP of Global Technology Services at Cornerstone OnDemand

"The REACH Framework is a fantastic, actionable structure to put in place to operationalize retention and expansion. Driving higher net retention and expansion are critical elements for every Customer Success team."

— **Laurence Leong,** Head of Account Management and Renewals at Jamf

"*REACH* is a quick read with concepts that are easy to grasp and digest. For Customer Success leaders and Chief Customer Officers seeking to drive revenue growth and strengthen customer relationships, this book gives you the roadmap to REACH your organization's North Star."

— **Marilyn Lin,** Founder of Lotus Group Intl and former CX leader at Salesforce and Delphix

"I am able to easily visualize the value of the REACH Framework and how I would implement it in my role. Adding a framework to expansion opportunities turns the thoughts that are floating around in the CSMs' heads into actionable ways to increase revenue."

— **Cory Black,** Manager of Customer Success Operations at NetDocuments

"I love that the book gives calls to action on how to implement REACH within my organization. The level of detail gives me just enough to be able to build a plan specific to my team. If you're in customer success and looking at expansion, this is the book to read."

— **Kristine Kukich,** CEO of The Training Sherpa and Trustee at CEdMA

"The book teaches people who consider themselves to be non-sales that it is their duty to uncover improvements to their customers' businesses that should result in sales opportunities."

— **Ben Collier,** Director of Professional Services at Freshworks

The Fastest Way to Drive Revenue Growth!

Share This Book With Your Employees to Get Everyone on the Same Page

Retail $24.95

Special Quantity Discounts

5-20 Books	$21.95
21-99 Books	$19.95
100-499 Books	$17.95
500-999 Books	$15.95
1,000+ Books	$13.95

Special Discount Pricing is subject to change.
Please contact us for final pricing options.

To Place an Order Contact:

rod@hellocco.com

Table of Contents

Read This First 1

Part 1 - The REACH Framework™ 7

The Challenge of Driving Revenue Growth 9
from Your Customer Base

Applying the REACH Framework™ 23

Part 2 - Implementing the REACH Framework™ 47

R – Relationships 49

E – Engagement 69

A – Actions 89

C – Customer Value 107

H – Horizons 123

Part 3 - Putting REACH into Action 137

Accelerate Your Expansion Growth with REACH 139

BONUS CHAPTER 161
How to Overcome Excuses and Start Using REACH

Your Next Steps 165

About the Author 167

The Ultimate Guide for CCOs and Aspiring CCOs! 169

Acknowledgments 179

Read This First

The roles of Customer Success teams and Account Management teams are at a critical junction. Companies across many industries, including technology, software, financial services, and healthcare, must focus on generating profitable, repeatable revenue growth. Surprisingly, many companies have not made this the primary focus over the past decade.

However, as interest rates rise and investors no longer value companies primarily as a multiple of revenue growth, boards of directors are demanding that executives find new strategies to generate revenue while improving profit margins. At the same time, many technology buyers, for example, face tighter investment budgets for new products and services, making it even harder for these technology companies to attract new clients. This increases the cost of acquiring new customers, creates longer sales cycles, and extends the payback period.

These circumstances leave CEOs and CFOs with no alternative but to ask their leadership teams to drive faster growth from existing customers. Your Customer Success or Account Management team often has the closest interactions with your current customers. Historically, expanding within your existing customer base has been a very cost-effective way to generate revenue growth. You have relationships with and access to decision-makers, understand customer needs, and can highlight the value you are already delivering to their organization.

This should be easy for Customer Success and Account Management teams. Unfortunately, many teams don't know how to drive this growth predictably and consistently. I wrote this book to address this situation.

Instead of writing a 300-page book that would take a long time to read, I have created a short book that is easy to understand and gets right to the point. I wanted to share this new framework with you as soon as possible so you can start implementing the approach I have used with great success across various industries.

I created *REACH* as a strategic tool to help transform the Customer Success and Account Management functions into strategic, revenue-generating powerhouses. This framework enables team members to seamlessly recognize and capitalize on expansion opportunities, fostering a more holistic approach to customer relationships that benefit customers and the company's bottom line.

How This Book Is Structured

This book has three parts:

Part 1: Introduction to the REACH Framework™ – We will explore the challenges facing Customer Success and Account Management leaders when expanding revenue growth from their customer base. You will see how the REACH Framework™ can help improve results. We will review the basics of REACH and then walk through the high-level steps an organization can take to apply this framework. This may be all you need to read if you are an executive. You should be able to get through this section in 30 minutes.

Part 2: Implementing the REACH Framework™ – Discover a practical guide that you and your teams can use to help systematically identify and capitalize on expansion opportunities with an existing portfolio of customers. This section also includes strategies for scoring customers based on the REACH Factors, creating a Growth Propensity Index™, and prioritizing accounts to uncover and nurture potential growth opportunities efficiently. If you work closely with customers, this part will be particularly relevant. You should be able to read this section in 30 minutes.

Part 3: Putting REACH into Action – Finally, we will discuss how to build REACH into your ongoing operations. I will give you a roadmap, so you can implement the REACH Framework™. I will walk you through the steps necessary to add rigor and structure, so you can feel more confident about your team's ability to achieve its expansion targets.

This section will resonate most if you are in a leadership or operations role (i.e., Revenue Operations, Sales Operations, Customer Success Operations). You should be able to cover this section in 30 minutes or less.

Tips for Reading This Book

In this book, you'll notice that I highlight critical insights, tips, and best practices to make it easier to recall and apply these principles. These tips are based on the experiences of hundreds of post-sale leaders, managers, and frontline team members as well as my own. You'll recognize these callouts quickly by these icons.

Expansion Accelerators -- Expansion accelerators highlight examples of insights, actions, and decisions that can improve your ability to grow revenue from existing customers. They may introduce you to new skills, suggest probing questions to ask, and recommend opportunities for interacting with key peers and customer stakeholders. Remember the game Chutes and Ladders you may have played when you were a kid? The "Expansion Accelerators" are the Ladders.

AI Insights – Artificial intelligence is pivotal in enhancing our strategies and outcomes. In these callouts, I highlight ways to leverage AI tools, data analytics, and predictive modeling. I demonstrate ways you can harness the power of AI, providing you with a competitive edge in identifying expansion opportunities, understanding customer behavior, and making data-driven decisions.

Metrics That Matter – A critical trend is the growing role that Customer Success and Account Management teams play in increasing company revenue and profitability. You will learn examples of how you and your organization can measure outcomes to demonstrate the value you provide to your customers and the impact your organization has on company performance.

Trends to Watch – I point out specific areas in which change is occurring or innovative ideas are developing. You should pay particular attention to these changes to determine how they could impact your business.

At the end of each chapter, you'll see a short set of questions to consider as you develop your action plan for each topic. You can use these questions as prompts for yourself or as discussion starters with your team or manager. Following the recommendations for specific steps allows you to develop the processes and skills you will need to drive predictable, repeatable expansion revenue growth. You also get access to worksheets, resources, and frameworks. Feel free to write directly in this book.

I hope that you find this book a convenient resource to help you navigate your opportunity to contribute to the growth of your organization while also developing your career. The role of Customer Success and Account Management teams is changing. I hope the REACH Framework™ and the strategies you learn from this book can be your trusted companion on your career journey. Let me know how it goes.

Rod Cherkas
April 2024
San Mateo, CA
rod@hellocco.com
www.rodcherkas.com

Part 1

The REACH Framework™

The Challenge of Driving Revenue Growth from Your Customer Base

The Reality of Expansion Revenue Today

Picture yourself in the boardroom of almost any technology company. Charts and data flash on the screen, setting the stage for the sales and marketing leaders. You will likely hear the VP of Sales say something like, "We are not meeting our sales goals. The Customer Success department is a drain on our resources and is not contributing enough to our sales growth. We should cut some Customer Success resources and hire more salespeople."

That sales leader is wrong, and I'm here to tell you why.

There is a huge opportunity we are missing and that we rarely talk about – leveraging your existing customer base. We are leaving millions of dollars of expansion revenue on the table. The best way to expand revenue is through your Customer Success or Account Management functions. Why?

Because your customers already trust those teams and value your solutions. There is immense potential here, and you are not taking advantage of that opportunity. These teams can help you expand your business.

So instead of cutting back on your Customer Success or Account Management efforts, invest in these teams and recognize them as the huge potential revenue source they are.

The urgency to adopt such an approach has never been greater. Companies now find themselves at a crossroads. They can continue focusing primarily on generating new sales or pivot towards maximizing the existing customers' revenue potential. The latter is where your Customer Success and Account Management teams, armed with the right tools and framework, can become heroes.

I created the REACH Framework™ to help solve this problem.

The REACH Framework™ centers around the concepts of Relationships, Engagement, Actions, Customer Value, and Horizons. It provides an operating system for your teams to tap into this potential in a repeatable, predictable way. This framework is not about morphing your teams into salespeople. It's about enhancing their roles to naturally uncover and pursue expansion opportunities in alignment with customer-centric values.

In a recent research report called *ScaleUp by the Numbers* published by Insight Partners, a growth investment firm that has invested in over 800 companies, the report found that only 19% of technology companies surveyed have documented processes for generating expansion revenue in their portfolio. This compares to 86% of companies that have documented processes for customer onboarding and 68% for conducting renewals. You can see this is a systemic challenge, not just a problem for you and your company.

TRENDS TO WATCH: Only 19% of companies surveyed had documented processes for generating expansion revenue which is why many are failing in their expansion efforts.

In working with clients, speaking with hundreds of leaders, and reviewing board presentations at dozens of companies over the past few years, I've observed that only a small fraction of a company's time and resources is spent on growing revenue from current customers.

Meanwhile, at no time in the past 30 years has there been a more critical need from your C-Suite and Board to grow revenue faster from your existing customer base.

Why is growing expansion revenue so important now?

Many company valuations have plummeted. Technology buyers are critically evaluating their spending decisions. More actively than ever before, companies' procurement departments engage in tough sales negotiations with you.

For these reasons and more, generating new sales bookings from prospects has been slow, expensive, and often disappointing.

Increasing top-line revenue comes primarily from two sources: finding new customers or growing existing ones. If new-customer acquisition slows, companies need to fill the gap. Executives are now pinning their hopes on leveraging current customer relationships to stimulate growth, improve profitability, hit bookings targets, and conserve cash.

Your board members may wonder why your customers, who may be highly satisfied with your solutions, aren't increasing investment in your solutions. Customer Success and Account Management teams are well-positioned to identify, nurture, and often close those opportunities. But if these departments cannot demonstrate they can be counted on to deliver these results, your company's leadership is going to make changes.

Think of how many direct customer interactions your Customer Success Managers or Account Managers have. Twenty each week? Now extend this across 45 or more work weeks a year. That's almost a thousand chances a year for your team members to deepen their relationships, demonstrate value, learn about additional ways your customers can benefit from your solutions, and explore customers' expansion potential. More than likely, this work is turning into a thousand missed opportunities per team member per year.

So why isn't all that valuable insight you gather turning into revenue growth?

In my conversations with clients and other leaders in post-sale roles, I encounter a range of hesitations and misconceptions regarding their roles in driving expansion revenue:

- "Suggesting additional products might jeopardize my customer's trust."

- "I don't have the right skills or training to handle expansion conversations."

- "It is difficult to prioritize which of my customers have growth potential."

- "We are trusted advisors. Our customers don't want us to sell to them."

- "Selling is the sales team's responsibility."

- "I am not incentivized to identify growth opportunities."

- "I fear being too salesy and hurting my relationship with my customer."

- "I am overwhelmed with my current workload."

Do any of these ring a bell for you?

TRENDS TO WATCH Customer Success and Account Management leaders need to adapt their mindset and objectives to meet the future needs.

I have observed how leaders try – and often fail – to expand revenue growth. They changed an incentive, tracked Customer Success Qualified Leads, tweaked the job profile, or replaced a manager. They expected that expansion bookings and Net Revenue Retention would turn around or grow faster. Those tactics alone are not enough.

Introducing the REACH Framework™

I developed the REACH Framework™ to help you expand revenue growth from your current customer base. REACH provides an operating system that offers structure and improves the capability of Customer Success Management and Account Management teams.

REACH isn't about transforming those functions into sales teams. This framework is about enriching their roles with processes, skills, and strategic capabilities that contribute more directly to business growth. REACH is about recognizing and acting upon expansion opportunities that feel natural to their customer-focused approach.

REACH is a framework that creates revenue-generating powerhouses that are strategic and measurable.

For decades, sales organizations have used frameworks and methodologies like MEDDICC, Sandler®, SPIN, and Challenger to help optimize how they drive the sales pipeline, monitor progress, forecast outcomes, and deliver results.

REACH brings a level of rigor and predictability, empowering your teams to unlock and maximize expansion opportunities. Now, you will finally have a framework to achieve the outcomes required for your future success.

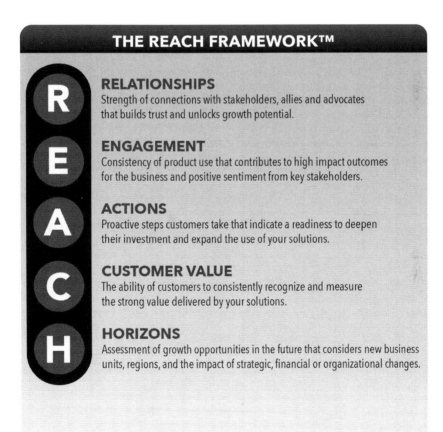

THE REACH FRAMEWORK™

R — RELATIONSHIPS
Strength of connections with stakeholders, allies and advocates that builds trust and unlocks growth potential.

E — ENGAGEMENT
Consistency of product use that contributes to high impact outcomes for the business and positive sentiment from key stakeholders.

A — ACTIONS
Proactive steps customers take that indicate a readiness to deepen their investment and expand the use of your solutions.

C — CUSTOMER VALUE
The ability of customers to consistently recognize and measure the strong value delivered by your solutions.

H — HORIZONS
Assessment of growth opportunities in the future that considers new business units, regions, and the impact of strategic, financial or organizational changes.

Each factor that makes up REACH is an indicator that contributes to predicting a customer's propensity to expand their investment with you. The framework also gives you a roadmap for working more closely with your customer to increase the likelihood of growing the relationship. You can track and monitor where your customers stand on these five dimensions and then actively work to move them further along.

Here is a high-level overview of the five factors in REACH. In the following chapters, more details are revealed about each factor so you can apply this approach to your business. You can also download a one-page cheat sheet about REACH on my website, rodcherkas.com/resources.

Each factor that makes up REACH is an indicator that contributes to predicting a customer's propensity to expand their investment with you. The framework also gives you a roadmap for working more closely with your customer to increase the likelihood of growing the relationship. You can track and monitor where your customers stand on these five dimensions and then actively work to move them further along. I'll introduce an approach to help you apply REACH to listen for expansion opportunities, nurture these opportunities with your customers, and move them toward closure. Each factor is critical in identifying and fostering opportunities for account growth within your existing customer base.

Here is a high-level overview of the five factors in REACH. In the following chapters, more details are revealed about each factor so you can apply REACH to your business. You can also download a one-page cheat sheet about REACH on my website, rodcherkas.com/resources.

R - Relationships

This element focuses on the strength and depth of connections with key stakeholders, allies, and advocates within the customer organization. Building trust and understanding mutual goals are fundamental in this step, laying the groundwork for future expansion conversations.

E - Engagement

Engagement refers to how deeply and consistently your customers interact with your product or service. Engagement is about understanding customers' usage patterns, their sentiment, and how critical your solution is to their business operations. This factor considers how your product or service aligns with their business outcomes. High engagement is often a precursor to expansion opportunities.

A - Actions

This component highlights the proactive steps customers take that can indicate their readiness for deeper investment and broaden the use of your solutions. These actions can range from inquiries about additional features, the desire to apply your solution to new use cases, hiring other team members, launching new products, and sharing feedback that signals interest in expanding their use of your solutions.

C - Customer Value

Here, the focus is on the measurable and qualitative benefits customers gain from your solutions. Understanding and articulating this value is critical in demonstrating to customers how further investment in your services can lead to even greater returns.

H - Horizons

This element assesses growth opportunities in the future (on the horizon) for your customers. Looking at the future in this way encourages looking beyond immediate needs to evaluate broader opportunities. It involves understanding customers' long-term goals, strategic direction, and potential areas for growth that your solution can support. This growth often requires expansion into other business units, regions, or newly-acquired companies and requires exploring the impact of strategic, financial, or organizational changes.

What Got You Here Won't Get You There

This is your call to action. The expectations for your job are changing, and you need to change with them. Over the past 25 years, I have watched other functions undergo fundamental transformations to meet evolving business needs and expectations. The Customer Success and Account Management functions are at a similar inflection point.

Consider the early 2000s. At that time, sales teams needed to completely alter how they operated. Before that, salespeople

REACH CHEAT SHEET – DEFINITIONS AND KEY QUESTIONS

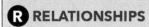 **RELATIONSHIPS** — Strength of connections with stakeholders, allies, and advocates that builds trust and unlocks growth potential

- Who are the key advocates, allies and decision-makers with whom you have established trust?
- How strong is the current relationship between your team and the customer's organization?
- Who are the advocates and allies at your customer who will champion your solution?
- Is there an executive at your company that is actively engaged?
- What relationships need to be nurtured in the future? What relationships are you missing?

 **ENGAGEMENT** — Consistency of product use that contributes to high impact outcomes and positive sentiment

- How frequently is your solution being used?
- Is it being used for multiple use cases? How could it be used more broadly?
- Is your customer leveraging and exploring many current features, capabilities, and benefits?
- How is your solution integrated into your customer's operational processes?
- What is the customer's sentiment about your solution and your company?
- What feedback have you received from users and key stakeholders about your solution?

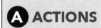 **ACTIONS** — Proactive steps customers take that indicate a readiness to deepen their investment and expand the use of your solutions

- What proactive steps has your customer taken that indicate an interest in a deeper investment?
- Does the customer have a history of growing their spending with you?
- Is there an upcoming renewal that creates an opportunity to discuss growth opportunities?
- Has the customer requested information about additional features, licenses, offerings, or services?
- Are there recent strategic initiatives or projects where your solution is playing a key role?
- Is your customer sharing results internally with executives, at staff meetings, or all-hands?

 **CUSTOMER VALUE** — Ability of customers to consistently recognize and measure the strong value delivered by your solutions

- How does your customer measure the value of your solution to their business?
- What metrics or KPIs have improved as a result of using your solution? Are the results impactful?
- How do you quantify the value of your solution to your customer's business results?
- In what ways has your solution contributed to the customer achieving their business goals?
- Can you identify examples of high-impact outcomes your customer has achieved?
- How does the value your customer achieves compare to the investment they make in your solution?

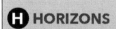 **HORIZONS** — Assessment of future growth opportunities that considers new regions, business units, use cases, and the impact of strategic, financial, or organizational changes

- Are there new business units or regions that could benefit from your solution?
- How do recent or upcoming strategic, financial, or organizational changes impact growth opportunities?
- Are there additional use cases where your solutions could help your customer achieve additional value?
- Are there mergers, acquisitions, or expansions planned that could create a new need for your solution?
- Is there budget available for any expansion investment?

used to go through a phone book, call prospects, try to get them into a meeting, and follow up in a very in-person way. With the growing proliferation of the internet and CRMs such as Salesforce and Microsoft Dynamics, prospects were becoming more educated about potential solutions as they gathered detailed information online before even engaging with a company's sales contact. The sales function changed.

Now, consider what happened to marketing. Decades ago, top marketers came from companies like Proctor & Gamble, Colgate, and Madison Avenue advertising agencies. Marketers were interested in generating brand awareness and focused on television, radio, billboards, and print journalism. Then boom! The internet and social media changed everything. Guess what? Marketers needed to evolve their strategies and skills to become more data-driven and internet-savvy. They would learn to leverage new solutions like HubSpot, Eloqua, and Marketo (where I worked) to nurture potential customers and communicate with existing ones.

Today, the Customer Success and Account Management functions are at similar inflection points. The role of CSMs and Account Managers needs to evolve. They have traditionally focused on ensuring customer satisfaction, adoption, and retention. Now, executive teams need these roles to transform into essential contributors to revenue growth.

TRENDS TO WATCH — Marketing and Sales have undergone fundamental transformations. Customer Success is at a similar inflection point.

Transitioning from a purely relationship-focused role to one that contributes significantly to revenue generation requires a change in mindset and providing more tools and processes to Customer Success teams. Roderick Jefferson is the VP of Go-To-Market Enablement at Siteimprove, wrote the best-selling book, *Sales Enablement 3.0*, and is an award-winning keynote speaker. He believes, "What CSMs and Account Managers are doing is too important not to have a consistent process." He adds, "There is a universal need for a framework like this across industries and verticals."

The good news is that you are likely in an excellent position to take advantage of this opportunity, positioning yourself and your team to drive business growth, and demonstrate the increased value of your organization to the company.

REACH is designed to help you and your teams accelerate this transition. In the next chapter, we will discuss how you can apply REACH in your business.

CHAPTER REVIEW

 QUESTIONS TO CONSIDER

- Which results of the REACH Framework™ resonate with you?
- How would your team benefit from a structured framework for growing your existing customers?
- What challenges does your organization confront when considering how to expand revenue from your existing customers?
- What changes in mindset, skills, and experience do you want to develop that will enable you to continue to grow your career?

 ACTION PLAN

- With your manager, discuss the benefits of having the REACH structured framework for expanding your company's relationships with existing customers.
- List any hesitations you have about contributing more to the growth of existing customers, such as, "I don't like to sell," or, "The sales department should handle this." Consider changing your mindset and developing new skills to overcome these hesitations.
- Identify two to three skills or experiences you would like to develop that will help you improve your capabilities and succeed in your current and future roles.

Applying the REACH Framework™

We will go through several simple steps to apply REACH in the following chapters.

1. Assess the readiness of your customers for expansion and additional investment.

2. Prioritize the customers on which to focus your expansion efforts.

3. Uncover expansion opportunities within these high-growth-potential accounts.

4. Develop an account expansion plan for nurturing the customer toward this future investment.

5. Execute a close plan to drive this opportunity to completion.

6. Track and measure your results with the REACH Customer Expansion Waterfall.

Let's take a quick look at the steps to applying this framework.

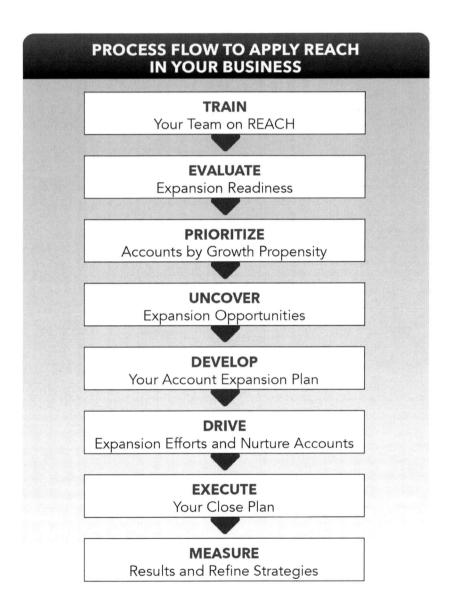

Assess the Readiness of Your Customers for Expansion

This initial step helps you evaluate your customers' current state and potential openness to expansion. This evaluation involves an analysis of the various factors described in the REACH Framework™: Relationships, Engagement, Actions, Customer Value, and Horizons. This assessment helps gauge your customers' existing situation, future needs, and how your solutions can continue to support their growth.

Qualitatively, you can identify strengths and weaknesses among these dimensions. You will find more details about how to do this evaluation in later chapters. You can also create a quantitative approach to measure where each customer stands on these five criteria. You will use these inputs to score each customer on the five factors to assign a combined score for what I call the Growth Propensity Index™ (see page 30 for an example). This score enables you to identify the relative potential for expansion opportunities compared to other customers or groups of customers.

Each business needs to develop its approach to scoring each factor to ensure consistency across the organization. Later in the book, there are examples of starting points for defining evaluation criteria for customers along each factor.

The Growth Propensity Index™ helps you assess and prioritize your customer's readiness for expanding their investment with your company.

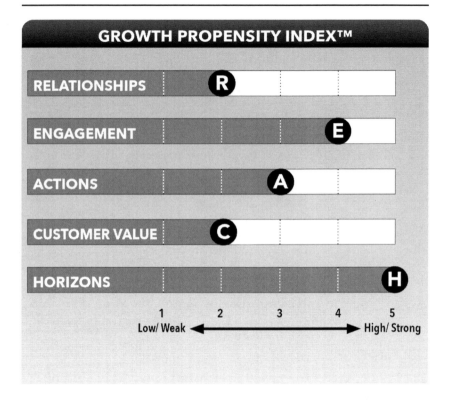

Some of my clients choose to capture this information in their CRM solutions, such as Salesforce or Microsoft Dynamics, or their Customer Success platforms, such as Gainsight, ChurnZero, Catalyst, Totango, or Vitally. Documenting this data enables broad visibility of your assessment and provides an easy way to track, monitor, and update information as your results and observations change.

Here's an example of what REACH documentation might look like in Salesforce.

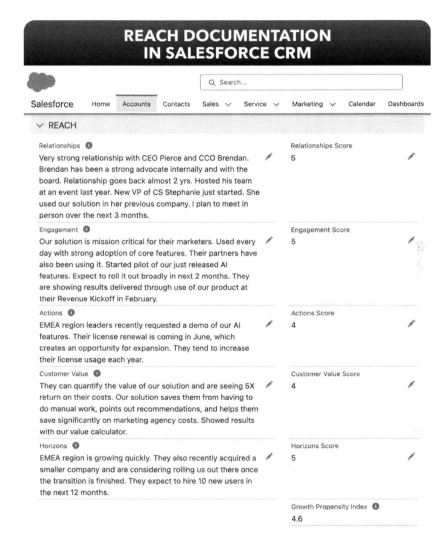

Prioritize Which Customers to Focus on with the Growth Propensity Index™

Imagine having a crystal ball that could tell you which customer relationships would likely yield expanded business opportunities. That's the essence of the Growth Propensity Index™ (GPI). By evaluating each customer against the REACH Factors, the GPI provides a composite score that ranks your customers based on their potential for expansion. A higher GPI indicates a greater likelihood that the customer is ready for further investment in your solutions.

In addition to prioritizing accounts, the GPI also helps focus energy and resources for maximum impact. This scoring system not only aids in managing expansion efforts but also in developing actionable strategies to foster customer relationships conducive to growth.

I collaborate with clients to customize this methodology for their unique business needs. This process involves developing a tailored scoring system that aligns with their specific business requirements. This approach equips their Customer Success or Account Management teams with a structured and rigorous process for prioritizing and engaging with accounts, enhancing CSMs' capability to strategically identify and cultivate those with the most significant potential for future growth.

EXPANSION ACCELERATOR — Prioritize your accounts so you can spend your time on customers with the most growth potential.

This assessment and prioritization process also helps you identify customers that are not quite ready for expansion and provides insight into how best to nurture those companies and relationships, so they become stronger candidates for growth in the future. You are also likely to identify customers who may never be good candidates for growth. This is helpful to know so you don't waste time trying to upsell and cross-sell to customers with no expansion potential.

Here's an example of what your account prioritization with REACH might look like in Salesforce.

ACCOUNT PRIORITIZATION BY GROWTH PROPENSITY INDEX™ IN SALESFORCE CRM

#	Account Name	Growth Propensity I...	Relationships Score	Engagement Score	Actions Score	Customer Value Score	Horizons Score
1	Sendoso	4.6	5	5	3	5	5
2	Knak	4.6	5	5	4	4	5
3	Algolia	4.0	4	5	4	4	3
4	Building Engines	3.2	5	3	2	5	1
5	Lakeside Software	2.2	3	3	2	2	1
6	Candex	2.0	2	3	1	2	2
7	VergeSense	1.6	2	2	1	1	2

My clients appreciate this process's rigor because it offers a more data-driven way to choose where to spend time with customers when trying to drive expansion opportunities.

Build REACH into your CRM or Customer Success Platform to improve visibility, tracking, and communication.

"REACH provides metrics-driven insight into how the account is doing and its growth potential," says Carly Bell, the Head of Customer Success at VergeSense. She continues, "That helps us focus on which accounts we should be paying attention to and which ones we shouldn't bother with."

REACH also gives teams specific action items to work on with customers. For example, the CSM or Account Manager can focus on developing internal champions or executive relationships for customers with a lower Relationship Score. If the Customer Value score is low, you can focus on building ways to measure, demonstrate, and communicate value.

Uncover Expansion Opportunities for High-Propensity Accounts

With a clear understanding of which customers have the highest growth potential, the next step is to uncover and nurture specific expansion opportunities within these accounts. This involves actively listening to your customers during

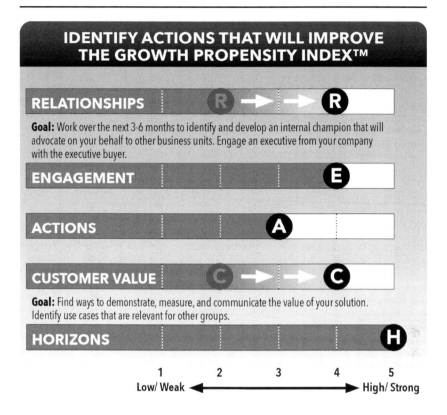

each interaction, asking questions to better understand their evolving needs, and leveraging your relationships to reveal current business challenges and future strategies. To help you understand your customers' needs, download a list of potential-probing questions to ask your customers from my website, rodcherkas.com/resources.

This stage of applying REACH often capitalizes on the many potential interactions you and your team may have with customers, such as one-on-one meetings, brainstorming sessions, email or Slack exchanges, business reviews, on-site visits, and product training. Because of your strong personal relationships, your customers are more likely to be open and transparent with you about their current state, evolving needs, and challenges.

"The ability of our CSMs to uncover expansion opportunities today is very personality-driven," says Nathan Jones, VP of Customer Operations at cybersecurity company Synack. He continues, "We have some people who are excellent at it. However, it isn't based on any structured approach. This framework adds that rigor for the whole team."

This step is where you can also leverage your ability to interpret trends and insights from your customers' current usage trends, past expansion behaviors, and other patterns you see among similar types of customers. This is where your partnership with your operations or data analytics teams can pay dividends.

For example, I run workshops with my clients where we identify topics and questions that CSMs or Account Managers can listen for in their interactions with their customers. This very interactive training process allows team members to practice listening and inquiry skills. We role-play, asking different questions to dig deeper into a customer's needs and business challenges. We talk about how to ask open-ended questions, probing questions, and diagnostic questions. We also cover how to apply active listening to those conversations. This exercise demonstrates how CSMs and Account Managers are uniquely positioned to gather information helpful in identifying future expansion opportunities.

 Ask probing questions, open-ended questions, and diagnostic questions to uncover expansion opportunities.

Alongside the various methods of uncovering expansion opportunities, you can also conduct a "whitespace" analysis to map out untapped or underleveraged areas within your customer's business that your solutions could address. This "whitespace" represents the potential business that could be yours if your existing customer fully utilized your suite of products and services.

Because of the customer's trusting nature in the CSM-client relationship, your contacts are commonly open and honest about their usage, results, challenges, and organizational barriers.

At a recent workshop with a company that makes software for the Artificial Intelligence (AI) industry, Julia, a CSM, shared that she developed such a strong partnership with her power-user that he invited her to join the customer's company-wide Slack group to interact more easily. This gave her unprecedented visibility to the customer's leadership structure, key contacts in other potential business units, and how the customer's teams were organized. The customer also consistently shared his challenges with Julia and valued her strategic insights into their mutual success. Julia used these conversations and the knowledge of other potential business lines to identify and lead discussions regarding high-value expansion opportunities.

Develop an Account Expansion Plan for Nurturing Your Customer Toward Additional Investment

An old commercial for Reese's Peanut Butter Cups makes an essential point about the value of collaboration between the Customer Success teams, Account Management teams, and their sales organization counterparts to drive expansion sales. In the commercial, two people are walking along a crowded city street. One is munching on a chocolate bar, and another is eating peanut butter out of a jar. They smash into each other as they turn a corner and accidentally discover the great taste of eating chocolate and peanut butter together.

When I think of CSMs and sales teams working together to grow accounts, I picture the CSM saying, "Hey, you got your chocolate in my peanut butter!" and the sales team member quips back, "You got your peanut butter on my chocolate!"

Companies that reinforce the need for strong collaboration between CSM, Account Management, and sales teams will likely achieve much better expansion results. This behavior leverages the strengths that each of those teams bring. You may even want to put specific metrics and incentives in place to encourage this cross-functional collaboration.

Aligning incentives and structuring compensation plans to reward expansion efforts is crucial. When Customer Success Managers and Account Managers are motivated not just by customer health metrics but also by their impact on revenue growth, it generates behavior to proactively seek expansion opportunities. This alignment ensures that their personal success is tied to the company's growth, driving a powerful incentive for expansion.

In applying REACH, CSMs and Account Managers play a pivotal role in laying out the path of an Account Expansion Plan or a Joint Account Expansion Plan. Their close relationships with customers put them in a unique position to identify early signs of potential growth and readiness for further investment. These professionals are often the first to spot new use cases, increased engagement, or other indicators that a customer is primed for expansion.

Once a potential expansion is identified through this process, you will want to make sure that the opportunity is appropriately documented in your company's CRM system and assigned to the appropriate owner for follow-up. In some cases, you may be the opportunity owner. In other cases, the owner may be a colleague from your sales team.

Recognizing that not all CSMs and Account Managers may drive the entire commercial cycle from identification to contract close, this step emphasizes the importance of effective collaboration with their sales team counterparts. This partnership ensures a seamless transition to help close deals.

This partnership ensures a seamless transition to help close deals.

The collaboration involves regular communication, strategy meetings, and sharing insights and updates about the customer's evolving needs, preferences, and potential obstacles. These interactions should focus on aligning the strategies of both teams, ensuring that the handover of information is smooth, and that the sales account executive has all the necessary context to engage with the customer effectively.

Effective communication channels between CSMs, Account Managers, and Sales Account Executives are essential. This could involve setting up regular check-ins, using shared digital platforms for updates, or establishing formal processes for transition and handover. The key is maintaining an open, ongoing dialogue that allows for real-time updates and adjustments to the account strategy.

As part of collaborative planning, CSMs and Account Managers should prepare comprehensive account briefs that include detailed insights about the customer's history, current use cases, potential areas for expansion, and any specific customer sentiments or preferences that could impact the sales process. This preparation ensures that even if a sales account executive steps in, they are not starting from scratch but building upon a foundation of deep customer understanding.

 Document and share your insights about your customer's expansion potential with relevant internal stakeholders.

Execute Your Expansion Close Plan

To drive the process of closing a new sale, Sales Account Executives have long leveraged a structured approach often known as a "close plan" to steer the journey of converting prospects into customers. This approach is invaluable for optimizing the sales process. The close plan enhances efficiency by systematically reducing the time required to close each sale. It also helps anticipate and mitigate potential obstacles. Providing a clear roadmap aligns efforts, focuses on key decision points, and ensures consistent engagement with prospects so you can streamline your path to a sale.

The concept of an "Expansion Close Plan" for Customer Success Managers and Account Managers emerges as a helpful parallel to more efficiently close expansion deals. This plan outlines action items designed to address customer needs, demonstrate product value, paint the picture of how the company can benefit from your solution, answer questions, resolve potential roadblocks, and ultimately secure a signed contract. It also helps prevent last-minute challenges and prepares the customer for what happens after the sale. You can find a sample template for an "Expansion Close Plan" on my website, rodcherkas.com/resources.

Leveraging an "Expansion Close Plan" process can provide value in the four ways discussed here.

Predictability and Structure

Much like how a close plan used with prospects brings a degree of predictability and structure to acquiring new clients, the Expansion Close Plan offers a level of rigor and a systematic approach to expanding existing accounts. Your leadership and finance organization will value your ability to forecast results more accurately than in the past.

Tailored Strategy

Each plan is tailored to the customer's specific context, considering that client's history, current usage, and future potential. This ensures that the expansion strategy is aligned with the customer's evolving needs and growth trajectory. Even when you start with a close plan template, you can easily update this template to meet the needs of your customer's situation.

Systematic Approach

The Expansion Close Plan offers a step-by-step approach to nurturing and developing opportunities within existing accounts, making upselling or cross-selling more streamlined and effective. The plan enables new team members in your organization to quickly learn and ramp up their productivity so that your company can benefit from their outcomes more quickly. Following this approach also allows existing team members to apply best practices that have worked well in other parts of your organization.

Improved Collaboration and Coordination

This plan fosters closer collaboration between CSMs, Account Managers, Sales Account Executives, and other organizational stakeholders, such as your finance, legal, and IT teams. While each has distinct roles and processes, the Expansion Close Plan ensures all parties are aligned in their approach and timing related to customer growth.

The REACH process works equally well in situations where CSMs or Account Managers own both the opportunity identification and close process. It also works well in situations where CSMs own only the early stages and then hand the deal to the sales team to close.

Track and Measure Results with the REACH Customer Expansion Waterfall and an Expansion Impact Dashboard

You need to define a way to track and report your forecasts, manage your pipeline, and share results related to your expansion efforts. When I work with clients, I recommend building these results into an Expansion Impact Dashboard.

This dashboard can include reports and visualizations related to the topics listed here.

- List of customer accounts prioritized by their Growth Propensity Index™

- Segmentation of accounts with high, medium, and low propensity to expand

- REACH scoring and notes for customer accounts

- Pipeline and forecast of open expansion opportunities

- List of closed-won expansion opportunities

- Links to Expansion Close Plans for open expansion opportunities

- Links to account plans for high-potential expansion accounts

In addition to the foundational elements of the REACH Framework, I'm introducing a new concept to guide Customer Success and Account Management teams through the process of generating expansion revenue — the REACH Customer Expansion Waterfall. This model outlines a progressive sequence of stages that systematically tracks customers with potential for growth. From the initial identification of a Customer Expansion Lead to the culmination with Closed-Won Expansion Business, this waterfall concept offers a structured and measurable way to track the progress of customers through your expansion process.

As you integrate these stages into your workflow, you can apply percentages to each stage that estimates the likelihood that the expansion opportunity will close. This gives you a way to more accurately forecast the expected bookings you will achieve from your expansion pipeline.

Outcomes You Can Expect to See

The introduction of a structured framework like REACH creates benefits both for your organization and your customers. Here are a few examples of the outcomes you can expect to see by implementing REACH.

1. **Higher Expansion Bookings:** REACH enhances your team's ability to generate more upsell and cross-sell bookings from existing customers. Structure and focus empower team members to close more deals efficiently.

2. **Increased Net Retention Rates:** A systematic approach to identifying and pursuing expansion opportunities not only helps retain customers but also drives upsells and cross-sells across those customers' businesses, enhancing customer lifetime value.

3. **Improved Forecast Accuracy and Predictability:** Implementing REACH introduces a rigorous process that yields more repeatable outcomes, enhancing forecast accuracy. This framework also fosters a consistent approach across your team, contributing to the overall predictability of business performance.

4. **Accelerated Time to Close:** Close collaboration in identifying and nurturing expansion opportunities enables quicker identification of customer concerns and barriers, allowing for more efficient resolution and faster deal closure.

5. **Faster Pipeline Turnover Rates:** As your CSM and Account Management teams become adept at the REACH process, they can more effectively pinpoint genuine growth opportunities, leading to a higher close rate in the expansion pipeline.

6. **Better Customer Experience:** One of the most significant impacts of REACH is the enhanced value and insights the framework provides to your customers. Far from being growth-driven, the framework enriches customer experiences with your solutions and company. REACH facilitates strategic alignment on desired outcomes, enables the creation of tailored solutions to meet evolving customer needs, and ensures that customers derive measurable value from current and future solutions.

7. **More Engaged Team Members:** REACH encourages a more dynamic and proactive work environment, leading to increased job satisfaction and engagement among team members. By involving your team members in strategic revenue generation, it elevates their roles, instills a sense of ownership, and aligns their efforts more closely with the company's growth objectives.

Looking Ahead

REACH marks a timely paradigm shift in how Customer Success and Account Management teams are perceived within their organizations. This framework moves away from viewing these teams merely as cost centers to seeing them as strategic assets capable of driving significant revenue growth. REACH equips teams with the mindset, tools, and confidence to identify growth opportunities within existing customer relationships and to capitalize on those opportunities effectively.

This chapter set the stage for a deeper exploration of each factor in REACH. It outlined how this innovative approach can transform the conventional role of Customer Success and Account Management by turning existing customer relationships into a powerful engine for revenue expansion.

The rest of the book provides more insights, strategies, and real-world applications that can revolutionize your company's approach to customer engagement and revenue growth.

In the next section, we will dig deeper into each factor of REACH. We will review how to apply REACH to assess each customer's unique position and potential for growth.

CHAPTER REVIEW

 QUESTIONS TO CONSIDER

- Do you have a way to prioritize accounts so you can focus your efforts on high-priority accounts? How could REACH help you do this more consistently?
- How do you listen for clues about how your customers could get more value from your solutions? How could you benefit from using a structured approach?
- How do you define your expansion account strategy? Who do you collaborate with internally to coordinate your plan?
- What improved outcomes could you and your organization achieve with a structured, repeatable process? How would your CEO and investors care about these results?

 ACTION PLAN

- Meet with your manager and team to identify how the REACH Framework™ could benefit your organization and decide how you could leverage the framework in your business.
- Define the outcomes that a structured framework could help improve and expand customer relationships. Then discuss those items with your executive team and finance leader.
- Work with your systems team to identify ways you could track and monitor your team's use of REACH. Consider how you could build the framework into your CRM or Customer Success Platform.
- Develop an action plan for starting to use REACH across your team. Decide whether you will try out the concepts with internal resources and personnel or enlist the help of third-party experts.

Part 2

Implementing the REACH Framework™

In this section of the book, we will discuss five key factors contributing to a customer's propensity to expand their company's investment in your solutions. This evaluation may include purchasing additional solutions for the part of the business you are currently working with. It could also include making decisions to expand the use of your solutions into other business units, regions, and use cases.

These five factors are relevant for two reasons.

First, you can leverage these factors to assess the current state of a customer's readiness or propensity to expand their investment in your solution, which I coined the Growth Propensity Index™ (GPI). I provide a framework to help you measure your customer's growth propensity according to these five factors. By considering these scores together, you can create a GPI that enables you to prioritize which accounts to spend your time on to drive growth in your business.

Second, by understanding the current state of your customers along these five dimensions, you can define specific action steps to address gaps and increase the likelihood that a customer will grow their business with you in the future. These factors also provide a practical framework to guide your ongoing interactions with your customer, making each interaction more purposeful and goal oriented.

R - Relationships

Now, we will focus on how relationships form the foundation for expanding growth and additional investment within a particular account. You will learn:

- Why relationships are essential for growing your business with a customer.

- How you can improve your relationships in a way that increases the potential for future growth.

- How to identify and nurture internal champions that can help you grow your business.

- How to score your customer on the Relationship factor in REACH.

- What you can do to move your customer to a higher Relationship Score.

- When engaging your senior leaders in discussions with your customers is useful.

I was recently talking to one of my clients who is the Customer Success leader for a company that makes software for auto dealers. I learned that there are a lot of mergers and acquisitions in my client's industry. He told me how a single-store account was acquired by a much larger company with 60 stores that were all using a competitor's software product.

You would think this would have created a situation where this one store would be asked to consolidate its software to the platform the other 60 stores were using. However, the general manager of the acquired dealership location loved my client's software, got a ton of value from it, and had a solid, trusting relationship with the Customer Success Manager.

As soon as the acquisition was announced, my client's Customer Success Manager heard about the deal and let the sales account executive know. The dealer's general manager vocally advocated moving the other 60 locations to my client's software platform. And over the next few months, the bigger company did just that! The decision of the larger company to transition its entire network of dealerships to my client's software solution stemmed from the solid foundation and trusting relationship established with the GM at the original, single-store dealership.

Deepen Key Stakeholder Relationships for Expansion

One of the most critical indicators of readiness for expansion is the strength and depth of your relationships with key stakeholders, allies, and advocates within the customer organization. These people are the pillars that will enable future business opportunities.

Building successful relationships goes beyond just identifying influencers and decision-makers. Relationship building is not solely about personal rapport or being liked. Merely having names listed as "executive buyer" or "internal champion" in your CRM is essential but doesn't automatically lead to growth.

A vital indicator of a strong relationship are the internal champions who actively support and endorse your solution within their organizations. This endorsement involves advocacy and being a reliable reference for others internally who could benefit from your offerings. Building this kind of trust is about deeply understanding the challenges, career goals, and definitions of success for your key contacts. Building these relationships entails uncovering the needs and expectations of the organization's influencers who have the power to influence strategic or investment decisions.

Nurture your customers into champions who advocate for your solution with their other business units and leaders.

When considering the strength of your Relationship as part of applying REACH, here are a few sample questions you can consider.

- Who are the key champions, stakeholders, budget-holders, and decision-makers at your customer's organization?

- How would you describe the current level of trust and engagement with those champions?

- Are there advocates or allies within the customer's organization who champion your solutions?

- Are key stakeholders unknown, disengaged, or actively dissatisfied?

- Is an executive from your company actively engaged with and known to the customer?

- What relationships need to be developed and nurtured in the future?

- What key relationships are you missing or are not that strong?

Understand the Landscape of Relationships, Stakeholders, and Influencers

Customer Success Managers and Account Managers are in a fantastic position to understand, nurture, and improve organizational dynamics due to the trusted and mutually beneficial relationships they form with customers. CSMs are often in the best position to assess the current situation and define actions that improve the customers' propensity to expand their relationship with your solution.

The journey to assess and deepen relationships begins with understanding how your customers decide about future investments and expansions. Who are the key stakeholders and decision-makers at your customer's organization? Who are the influencers that are consulted for expertise or are respected for their input? Who are the potential blockers that might stand in your way? Building these relationships is about understanding their influence, priorities, and pain points. This knowledge can be critical for developing a targeted expansion strategy. Understanding your customer's business also helps you build credibility as you develop the relationship.

How would you describe the current relationship between your team and the customer's organization? Is the relationship transactional or does it feel more like a strategic partnership? Being honest in your assessment is essential. No matter how friendly and cordial, a superficial relationship rarely leads to significant expansion.

Demonstrate Your Interest in Learning How Your Customers Use Your Solution

One of my clients makes barcode and scanning software to streamline inventory management, shipping, and in-store shopping. For years, the initial interactions between CSMs and most of their largest customers were purely transactional. Then, the leader of the CSM team decided to encourage the CSMs to travel and visit many of their key customers in person.

One of the CSMs, Jakub, spent several days on-site with his customer. He visited the customer's warehouse, rode along on truck delivery routes, and saw how his solution was used in the daily routine of the end-users. The CSM met with the customer's executives, power-users, and frontline team members who used his solutions. By working together over those few days, the CSM transformed the relationship by highlighting his value as a strategic partner who is invested in the customer's success.

Jakub demonstrated that he understood his customer's business and provided insights related to their challenges. This shift opened doors to discussions about additional services that wouldn't have been previously considered. A few days after the visit, the vice president for store operations at the company Jakub visited reached out and wanted to learn more about one of the new solutions that had been discussed.

Identify and Nurture Internal Champions

Seek to identify and nurture advocates or allies within the customer's organization. These individuals see the value of your solutions and are willing to champion your cause to others internally. Their advocacy is a powerful tool for expanding your footprint within the organization.

When I worked at Marketo, I observed a situation almost a decade ago that demonstrated the value of having a strong internal champion who can advocate for the broader expansion of a solution across multiple functional teams. Fresh from college, David Kreitter, an implementation consultant in my organization, discovered the little-known communication tool called Slack. David signed up for a small subscription for our team to quickly answer customer questions with other consultants in real-time. This solution worked incredibly well, saving the consultants time and frustration as well as enabling users to get immediate answers from their peers.

He quickly recognized Slack's broader potential for the company and championed the cause to take his case to the VP of IT. Through his advocacy, more teams across Marketo could collaborate effectively. From Slack's perspective, providing its solution more broadly in the company would generate significant expansion revenue. This story demonstrates how the power of even a single, vocal, and passionate champion can become a pivotal factor in driving growth.

Consider how your executive team would recruit and hire a new senior leader. Sure, the team would ask that candidate for a list of references. But often, recruiters do what they call "backdoor reference checks." This is a tactic for getting feedback on prospective employees by contacting people in the candidate's network not explicitly provided by the candidate.

In a sales cycle with a new prospect, your marketing teams might create case studies for the company website, and your sales team can share a list of existing customers specifically chosen to be used as references. However, your prospects may be skeptical of what they hear because they know that these customers were selected to provide positive stories about your solution.

This stumbling block is not true for your existing customers.

For example, when considering whether to expand relationships with your company into new business units, regions, or use cases, the decision-makers from those other teams often rely on their own "backdoor references." In this case, the reference feedback and input from those internal stakeholders who are already familiar with how your solution works at the company. You need to cultivate these advocates and allies into champions who will speak up loudly and favorably on your behalf when expansion opportunities are being considered.

Keep Your Buyers Engaged and Informed but Not Overwhelmed

Just as it is critical to have an internal frontline champion advocating for your solution, being familiar with the executive decision-maker is essential. You want to ensure this decision-maker is informed about how your solution is being used and the value that solution drives for his or her company. These leaders will know their company's strategic direction, operational challenges, and opportunities where your solution might be valuable. However, they are also likely to be busier and not as regularly engaged with your solution as others.

Of course, it would be great if your executive buyer participated in every business review and could confidently rattle off how your solution benefits their organization. But more importantly, you want your executive buyer to hear from his or her team members about how your solution delivers the expected value for the company. You can then create impactful opportunities to reinforce your company's perception and value through personal interactions with the executive buyer.

Maranda Dziekonski – the SVP of Customer Success at Datasembly, a market intelligence platform for brands and retailers – was previously the Chief Customer Officer at Swiftly. One of Maranda's experiences at Swiftly demonstrates how to engage executive buyers and underlines the power of consistently communicating value.

When Maranda started doing executive business reviews (ERBs) with one of her clients, a large municipality in Texas, only five people attended. However, as Maranda and her team consistently highlighted departmental successes and showcased collective wins, interest and attendance grew exponentially. Over time, these EBRs became a hub of engagement, attracting over 30 attendees and multiple department heads. Attendees lined the walls due to the lack of chairs in the boardroom. The EBRs turned into anticipated events where the client's team members looked good in front of their CEO and celebrated their achievements using Swiftly's solutions. "It made our champions look like rockstars internally," Maranda added.

Maranda's story demonstrates how an EBR, meticulously designed to highlight customer successes and potential growth paths, cemented the value of Swiftly's services and empowered internal champions to advocate for the solution. This is a great example of creating impactful opportunities to reinforce the company's perception and value with executive buyers. While the executive buyer may not always be directly involved, they will hear success stories from teams that echo the solution's benefits and value throughout the organization.

Encourage Senior Leadership Engagement from Your Company

How involved are your executives with your most important clients? An executive sponsor from your company can work wonders in elevating the relationship's status with your customer. Customers appreciate a sign of commitment and seriousness, especially in fast-changing industries. This sponsor also creates an opportunity for what may feel like peer-to-peer executive interactions.

I had a client who made software for machine learning operations teams where the CEO was directly involved in discussions with the SVP of engineering at the customer's company. My client's CEO was not involved in escalation management. The CEO wasn't engaged in quarterly business reviews. Instead, he periodically reached out directly to SVPs of Engineering at key customers to talk about industry trends, share observations about the competitive environment, and discuss strategic customer issues. Even short chats like this between your company's senior executives and your customers can pave the way for expanded engagements.

Invite your CEO and other senior executives to engage with key customers periodically, not just when there is a crisis.

To facilitate this high-level engagement, establishing a structured plan for your senior leaders is useful. For example, a cadence of quarterly outreach, planned and supported by your CSMs or Account Managers, can provide a consistent touchpoint without overburdening your executives' schedules. These meetings or communications can be strategically designed to discuss industry insights, customer-specific strategic initiatives, or future product developments. By having a clear agenda and objectives for each interaction, you enable your executives to engage meaningfully, demonstrating commitment and thought leadership to your customers. This approach also streamlines executives' involvement and makes it easy for them to know what is expected of them.

Establish and Nurture Future Relationship Opportunities

Finally, what potential relationships haven't been tapped into yet? Are there up-and-coming leaders within your client's organization with whom you can build rapport today? Are there additional power-users of your solution that will help provide you with a broader bench of advocates and allies in case one of your current champions leaves the company or moves to a new role? Identifying emerging influencers within a client's organization and investing in those relationships early on can bring you long-term benefits.

Expanding the number of relationships you have at the company also prevents you from becoming "single-threaded," a situation referred to when you may only have one strong contact. Instead of being dependent on a single person, you want to be "multi-threaded," where you maintain a wide number of connections. This will decrease your risk of losing your customer if that one contact leaves the company or is promoted into a different role.

For example, one of my clients in the real estate technology industry faced a challenge with a power-user who was disengaged and resistant, skipped critical meetings, avoided product training, and even campaigned for his segment of the business to abandon my client's solution. The situation turned a corner when a CSM discovered that an enthusiastic power-user from another client had recently joined the resistant user's company. The CSM was able to then redirect her engagement efforts toward nurturing the relationship with this new, more-enthusiastic team member, establishing a much more reliable path toward generating growth opportunities in the future.

Score the Quality of Your Relationships as It Relates to the Growth Propensity Index™

In each chapter dedicated to a REACH Factor, we use a simple scoring system to evaluate a customer's propensity for growth. This system assigns a score from 1 to 5 for each factor, assessing the strength of your relationship, level of engagement, and other key indicators within the REACH Framework™.

Here's how to use this scoring system.

1. **Assign Scores for Each Factor:** For each of your customers, assess them against the five REACH Factors—Relationships, Engagement, Actions, Customer Value, and Horizon. Rate them on a scale of 1 (poor) to 5 (excellent) based on the criteria provided for each factor.

2. **Understand That the Framework is a Guideline, Not Absolute:** Remember, this scoring isn't about achieving perfection. The framework is a tool to give you a quantifiable way to gauge an account's growth potential. It's more about the insights you gain in the process than about the exact number.

3. **Equal Weighting for Simplicity:** To keep things simple and actionable, each of the five factors should initially carry an equal 20% weighting in the overall score. This approach makes the process less daunting and more user-friendly.

4. **Option for Custom Weighting:** If you feel confident, you can adjust the weightings to better reflect the unique aspects of your business or industry. However, starting with equal weighting is recommended for ease of use.

5. **Use Scores for Prioritization:** Once you've scored your customers, use the scores to prioritize your accounts according to their growth propensity. Customers with higher scores represent greater potential for expansion and may warrant more focused attention and resources.

This scoring table is just a starting point. When I work with clients, we fine-tune the specifics to align more closely with their organization's characteristics. But even in its basic form, this tool provides valuable insights into where to focus your growth efforts. You can start off simply by tracking these scores in a Google Sheet or Microsoft Excel worksheet. Once you have the framework working repeatedly, you can then move it to a system like your CRM or Customer Success Platform.

AI may soon enable you to automatically assign a REACH score based on information in your systems.

As you determine how you would score your existing customers to identify their propensity for future growth and what you can do to improve that propensity, here are a few questions to consider.

- Who are the key advocates, allies, and decision-makers with whom you have established trust?

- How strong is the current relationship between your team and the customer's organization?

- Are there advocates and allies at your customer's organization who will champion your solution?

- Is there an executive at your company who is actively engaged with the customer?

- What relationships need to be nurtured in the future? What relationships are you missing?

Relationships – Scoring Methodology

1 - Poor (Minimal or No Established Trust)

- You have no plan for managing your customer relationships.

- Key stakeholders and decision-makers are unrecognized or ignored.

- Interactions are inconsistent, lacking any real substance or strategic focus.

- There's an absence of champions within the customer's organization advocating for your solutions.

- Executive engagement from your company is non-existent, potentially reflecting a lack of strategic commitment.

- There is no systematic approach to identifying or cultivating potential relationship development opportunities.

2 - Fair (Limited Trust and Weak Relationships)

- There is some identification of key stakeholders and decision-makers, but engagement is superficial.

- Relationships are transactional rather than strategic, with minimal established trust.

- There are few champions within the customer's organization. Their potential as allies is untapped.

- There is sporadic executive engagement from your company, which shows a lack of strategic intent.

- Awareness of the need for relationship development exists, but actions are reactive rather than proactive.

3 - Good (Moderate Trust and Developing Relationships)

- Key stakeholders and decision-makers are identified, and trust is beginning to form.

- Relationships show signs of evolving beyond transactional to more strategic interactions.

- A handful of customer advocates have been identified. Initial efforts are in place to leverage these relationships.

- Executives are engaged occasionally. Discussions align with strategic goals.

- You have developed processes and action plans to build and strengthen relationships.

4 - Very Good (Strong Trust and Active Relationships)

- Key stakeholders and decision-makers are well known. You have established trusting relationships.

- You have frequent strategic interactions that demonstrate mutual value and understanding.

- Several strong customer advocates actively support and endorse your solutions.

- Executives provide strategic relationship depth to key customer stakeholders.

- A strategic plan with clear objectives and tactics is in place to develop relationships.

5 - Excellent (Exceptional Trust and Deep Strategic Relationships)

- Deep engagement with key stakeholders and decision-makers is confirmed by high trust and alignment on strategic goals.

- The relationship is marked by meaningful, regular interactions that drive mutual success.

- Numerous committed advocates within the customer's organization strongly align with your value proposition and have made introductions to other parts of their business.

- Executives from your company are heavily involved, adding significant value to the relationship.

- An effective strategy is in place for adapting to the customer's changing needs.

CHAPTER REVIEW

 QUESTIONS TO CONSIDER

- Why is it essential to develop strong relationships with customer champions to grow their future business?

- What are the characteristics of your customers that have turned into expansion opportunities?

- What new ideas, skills, and techniques did you learn from this chapter that you can use to strengthen relationships with your customers?

- How do you consistently develop client champions who become internal advocates and are willing to recommend your services to their colleagues?

 ACTION PLAN

- Identify two to three customers with whom you have strong relationships. Make a list of what you have done to develop those relationships. Define the characteristics of the customer that made that relationship possible.

- Identify two to three customers with high potential for future growth but who don't have the strong relationships you need. Apply the concepts you learned in this chapter to define a strategy to improve the relationships.

- Score your accounts according to the methodology outlined at the end of the chapter. Identify opportunities to improve your relationships and increase your customers' propensity to invest more in your products or services.

- Use this plan/worksheet/questionnaire as input into prioritizing your accounts using the REACH process.

E – Engagement

The E in REACH™ is about delving deeper into how customers interact with your product and service. Engagement is a crucial indicator of customers' satisfaction and openness to expanding their commitment. You will want customers who consistently use your solution in a way that contributes to high-impact outcomes and positive sentiment. This section will dig into various aspects of customer engagement as a key component of REACH.

In this chapter, you will learn:

- What questions about engagement you can ask to assess your customer's propensity to grow.

- The value of quantifying the frequency and depth of how customers use your solutions.

- How a customer's exploration of new use cases and features can indicate a willingness to expand.

- How to listen for feedback that enables you to assess a customer's sentiment.

- The role that advocacy and internal promotion of your solution can play in your growth opportunities.

One of the clearest signs that your customers are ready for expansion is their level of engagement with your solution. If the individuals and teams at a company are not actively using and engaging with your product, this lack of engagement significantly diminishes the chances that they will deepen their investment or advocate for your solution's adoption across other departments. Lack of engagement is a red flag, indicating a missed opportunity for expansion and a potential risk for customer churn.

However, recognizing a lack of engagement can be a valuable early-warning sign and provides an opportunity for proactive intervention. This heads-up enables your team to take targeted actions to reengage these customers. You can tailor your approach by understanding the reasons behind the customers' low engagement – whether it's a lack of awareness of certain features, perceived complexity, or a misalignment with their needs. Initiatives such as personalized training sessions, user-friendly guides, or demonstrating the direct impact of your solution on the customers' business goals can reignite their interest and usage.

So, what do I mean by "engaged" in this context? When I work with my clients, I generally consider five areas. This chapter goes into more detail about these facets.

1. Quantifying usage frequency and depth

2. Broadening usage scenarios

3. Gauging customer sentiment

4. Generating adoption of new features and upgrades

5. Encouraging customer advocacy and promotion

Quantify Usage Frequency and Depth

Often, the first step is to consider how frequently and intensely your product is used within the customer's organization. This is not just about login frequency, although when logins or usage is zero, that fact can indicate a problem. This is about understanding usage patterns, identifying the most used capabilities, learning how customers expand their product maturity, and recognizing where the solution becomes indispensable to the organization. Customers with solid usage patterns in your current solutions will be more likely to consider additional cross-sell and upsell opportunities than customers who hardly use your solution.

Ideally, you want your solution to become habitual for your customers. You want your solution to be not just an option but the default choice for specific tasks or processes. When I worked at Intuit early in my career, co-founder Scott Cook often said that you want your products to be so easy that your customers would never think about going back to doing things the old way. For example, who would want to calculate taxes manually when you could use Intuit's TurboTax product? When thinking about your own customer's usage frequency and depth, consider how well your solution meets this standard.

When I led Marketo's customer enablement and education teams, one of our key objectives was driving product adoption and enhancing the skills of customers who were just starting out with our solution. We developed a customer maturity model that provided a structured framework for moving customers along the journey from basic to advanced usage. At each stage, we defined a particular set of features and benefits that customers could expect to use to demonstrate proficiency and engagement.

In the first and second stages of our maturity model, we focused on making sure that our customers were introduced to sticky features and benefits to get them to use capabilities that differentiated our solution from competitors. For example, we wanted to help customers set up nurture campaigns, lead scoring programs, and online seminar registrations using Marketo.

Once these programs ran, Marketo users found that these new automations made their lives easier and saved them vast amounts of time. We could gradually introduce them to a broader range of marketing programs they could automate and personalize with our solutions. These were undoubtedly high-impact benefits, but introducing these other capabilities also made users less likely to consider switching or going back to their old way of doing things. Teaching users these new features also made them eager to keep learning, finding new ways to provide automated, more personalized, and relevant messages to their customers while saving time.

We then could measure how often customers used Marketo, the number of nurture emails and campaigns executed, and the click-throughs to the customers' landing pages. We even built this into an analytics model that calculated a score based on customers' use of specific combinations of features. When engagement and activity were low, we could proactively see why usage was down and correct any problems to reengage the customer. When usage was high, we could continue encouraging customers to learn new capabilities and expand their investment. There are also several software solutions on the market, like Pendo, Mixpanel, Amplitude, UserIQ, and Gainsight, that can help you measure and analyze customer engagement.

Broaden Usage Scenarios

Are your customers leveraging your solution to its fullest potential? Are they using all the features and benefits that you offer? They might be unaware of the breadth of your product's capabilities. For example, all the information your team shared during an onboarding session might have overwhelmed your customers. Or they might not have realized one of your solutions could have solved one of their problems. Assessing how your solution is currently being used can reveal opportunities for upselling features that align with unexplored use cases. If your customers feel like they are not even using what they currently have, convincing them to buy more might be hard. Your team should let them know about relevant new features and benefits, so they continue to use your product and highly value your solution.

During a recent conversation, Rob Schmeltzer explained that during his time as the Senior Director of Customer Success at DocuSign, CSMs were trained to look for particular behaviors and situations that indicated opportunities to broaden use cases. One example he described was a situation where different teams of customers were responsible for new sales and renewals. "We often initially sold DocuSign to sales teams," he says, continuing, "They would start using it to get NDAs and contracts signed. They would quickly see how much time it saved them."

However, as the DocuSign CSMs learned more about their customers, they might discover that a different team handled the renewal contract, not the original sales team. Schmeltzer recalled, "This created an obvious expansion opportunity for us to grow our footprint to support a different use case." DocuSign would train its CSMs to uncover expansion opportunities by listening for certain behaviors and actions in common situations.

This factor assesses how widely your solution is applied across different areas of a customer's business. High scores in this area are characterized by customers not just using your product for its primary function but exploring and implementing your solution across varied use cases. This demonstrates your solution's relevance to different aspects of a customer's operation.

Gauge Customer Sentiment

Engagement also encompasses the customer's sentiment toward your solution. This can be gauged by direct feedback from surveys (i.e. CSAT, NPS, post-onboarding), the tone and words customers use in their electronic interactions with you, the frustration or positivity felt during support interactions, and general attitudes expressed during in-person discussions. Positive feedback, constructive criticism, and eagerness to explore new features are signs of healthy engagement. This sentiment can be a valuable source of information, indicating areas for improvement and potential expansion opportunities.

As you consider your customers' current sentiment and how to improve it. Ask these questions.

- What feedback are you receiving from your customers?
- How do stakeholders feel about your product?
- What issues are customers running into that you might correct from reviewing support cases?

- Does your customers' sentiment indicate that they would be supportive of expanding their relationship?

- In what areas would you need to improve to become more of an advocate for your solution?

- Are you hearing concerns that might indicate customers are talking to a potential competitor?

The growing use of AI-enabled solutions, such as ChatGPT, UpdateAI, Gong, Intercom, and Zoom, significantly enhances your company's ability to gather and interpret customer sentiment by efficiently analyzing large volumes of data from internal sources such as meeting transcriptions, customer feedback surveys, and support interactions as well as external sources such as social media posts, competitive review websites, and community forums. This advanced analysis can help you identify prevailing attitudes and trends reasonably accurately and provide actionable insights, enabling you to respond proactively to customer needs and trends.

AI-enabled solutions enhance your ability to interpret customer feedback and sentiment.

Generate Adoption of New Features and Upgrades

Adopting new features and upgrades is a crucial indicator of your customers' engagement with your product and is an essential prerequisite for them to expand their relationship with your company. When your team presents new solutions to your customers and those customers actively try out new functionality, their action shows they are looking to maximize the potential of your solution. It also demonstrates their curiosity to explore and learn additional ways that your product can help them. This behavior suggests a commitment to not just using but optimally leveraging your product in their operations.

For instance, consider a software solution that helps law firms manage, share, and collaborate on their documents and case files. Initially, this software might be used within one office to help the legal team keep track of its files electronically in organized, online folders. Later, the solution could integrate with their email systems, such as Microsoft Outlook and Office 365. Then, the use cases could expand to enable the lawyers to collaborate on documents easily with their clients, adding another benefit and set of sticky features.

For law firms that participate in trials, the software can make it easier to create documents that can be formatted into binders that the attorneys can use in court hearings. Finally, the lawyers in one office could tell lawyers in other regional offices how much easier this document management solution makes their lives, also telling lawyers in the other offices they should use the solution too.

This company developed a strategic, proactive sequence of activities to help its customers broaden their usage and explore new features.

This kind of engagement is about more than just using your product. It reflects a choice by the customer to grow and adapt. When customers incorporate new features into their workflow, your solution aligns with a broader range of long-term business goals. The engagement demonstrates that your product is an evolving part of how they achieve their business strategy.

Furthermore, customers' willingness to adopt new features often leads to more collaborative relationships. And collaboration opens opportunities for discussions about future needs and potential product enhancements. As customers explore and provide feedback on new features, they directly contribute to the improvement and development of your product. This deepens their investment in your solution and drives your product's evolution to better meet market needs.

Partnering with your product marketing and customer marketing teams can significantly amplify efforts to generate the adoption of new features and upgrades. Their expertise in crafting compelling messages can make a crucial difference in how these features are perceived and embraced by customers.

Encourage Customer Advocacy and Promotion

As we continue exploring the impact of customer engagement on growth propensity, we need to focus on the value of internal customer advocacy and promotion. This is where satisfaction and engagement with your solution turn into active, enthusiastic support for your product within your customer's organization. When customers are willing to take this step, it signals that they not only value your solution but are also willing to support your solution and publicly endorse your product. This level of engagement is a positive indicator of customers' growth propensity to expand your solution into other use cases, business units, teams, or regions.

Acknowledging the roles that you and your company play in fostering these activities is important.

Proactive creation of advocacy opportunities is not just a passive, wait-and-see approach. This activity can be a strategic initiative that companies undertake to empower their customers to become champions of your products. This proactive stance involves identifying potential advocates and providing them with platforms and contexts where their positive experiences and endorsements can be shared, both internally within their organizations and externally with the wider market. By doing so, companies can effectively transform satisfied customers into active promoters, amplifying the reach and impact of those promoters' advocacy.

Such advocacy takes various forms. Customers might recommend your product to other departments, remote offices, or professional networks. They might share their success stories or participate in case studies and testimonials. They might participate in your customer community or attend your user groups, webinars, and office hours. Their willingness to speak at your conferences, panel discussions, or events can also be a clear validation of trust in your solution. These actions reflect more than just using a product effectively. Your customers' participation shows an added level of engagement by championing your product within and beyond their organizations.

I have worked at several companies, including Marketo and Gainsight, where we organized large, annual user conferences that attracted thousands of customers and prospects. At those events, our customers often took the lead, facilitating dozens of sessions and engaging in numerous speaking opportunities. They shared their stories, best practices, and successes. It's my understanding that one key criterion for being selected was the likely potential for expansion growth within the speaker's company. This makes sense, as being a speaker not only demonstrates a commitment to the solution's success at his or her company but also highlights the speaker's organization as a prime candidate for future growth opportunities.

In addition, this level of advocacy not only benefits your company's growth potential but also provides significant advantages for the customer. Advocacy gives your customers

Invite your champions at high-potential expansion customers to speak at your webinars, conferences, and events.

a platform to elevate their professional brand, gain visibility with their executives, and showcase their strategic impact on their company's success. This engagement can often be a catalyst for their professional advancement. As they champion your solution, they simultaneously bolster their case for career growth.

This advocacy is crucial for generating expansion opportunities. Customers publicly endorsing your product strengthens their relationship with your company and amplifies your brand's credibility. These endorsements create a ripple effect, encouraging others within the promoters' organizations to adopt your solution more broadly. Additionally, their testimonials and case studies are powerful tools in convincing other business units or regional offices to consider your product. Customer advocacy fuels a cycle of trust and credibility, paving the way for further expansion and more profound business relationships.

Your marketing organization can also be a great cross-functional partner to help drive customer engagement, advocacy, and internal promotion. These teams possess unique insights into customer behavior, market trends, and effective communication strategies that can significantly enhance the identification and realization of growth opportunities.

By integrating the intelligence and resources from marketing efforts, CSMs and Account Managers can ensure a more targeted and cohesive approach to customer engagement and expansion. This partnership enables you to potentially leverage marketing campaigns, customer success stories, and tailored communications to reinforce the value proposition and uncover new avenues for expansion. This cross-functional collaboration not only amplifies the impact of expansion initiatives but also aligns the organization's goals towards a unified strategy for customer-centric growth.

Score the Quality of Engagement as It Relates to the Growth Propensity Index™

As you determine how to score your existing customers to identify their propensity for future growth and contemplate what you can do to improve that score, here are a few questions to consider.

- How frequently is your solution being used?

- Is your solution being used for multiple use cases? How could it be used more broadly?

- Is your customer leveraging many of the current features, capabilities, and benefits?

- Is your customer learning about and exploring new features and capabilities?

- What is the customer's general sentiment about your solution and company?

- What feedback have you received from users and key stakeholders about your solution?

Engagement – Scoring Methodology

1 - Poor (Minimal or Inconsistent Engagement)

- The product is rarely used within the customer's organization with minimal utilization of your solution's features and benefits.

- The solution is used for very few or no use cases, indicating a lack of integration into the customer's operations.

- There is little to no exploration of new features and capabilities by the customer.

- Feedback from users and stakeholders is either negative or non-existent, indicating a potential lack of engagement or dissatisfaction.

- The general sentiment about the solution and your company is hostile, negative, or indifferent.

2 - Fair (Limited Engagement)

- The solution is used occasionally but not consistently or broadly within the customer's organization.

- The solution is used only by a single user or for a limited number of use cases, with significant potential for broader application.

- Some features and benefits are utilized, but many still need to be explored or utilized.

- Feedback from users and stakeholders is mixed, with some positive aspects and notable areas of concern.

- The general sentiment about the solution and your company is neutral or slightly positive.

3 - Good (Moderate Engagement)

- The solution is used regularly, but there may be room for more consistent or broader usage.

- The solution is used for a few key use cases, with some exploration of additional applications.

- A good number of features and benefits are utilized, but there may be untapped potential in others.

- Feedback from users and stakeholders is generally positive, with some suggestions for improvement.

- The general sentiment about the solution and your company is positive, indicating a satisfactory level of engagement.

4 - Very Good (Strong and Diverse Engagement)

- The product is used frequently and consistently across multiple areas of the customer's organization.

- The solution is used for various use cases, demonstrating its versatility and integration into the customer's operations.

- Most features and benefits are actively utilized, with customers regularly exploring and adopting new capabilities.

- Feedback from users and stakeholders is very positive, with an appreciation for the solution's impact and value.

- The general sentiment about the solution and your company is very positive, reflecting strong engagement and satisfaction.

5 - Excellent (Exceptional and Impactful Engagement)

- The product is integral to the customer's daily operations. The solution is used extensively and strategically.

- The solution is leveraged for multiple use cases, demonstrating deep integration and essential value to the customer's business.

- Many features and benefits are fully utilized, with customers proactively seeking and embracing new functionalities.

- Feedback from users and stakeholders is overwhelmingly positive, often citing the solution as critical to their success.

- The general sentiment about the solution and your company is exceptionally positive, indicating a deep, strategic level of engagement and partnership success.

CHAPTER REVIEW

 QUESTIONS TO CONSIDER

- Why is understanding and measuring how deeply a customer engages with your solutions important?
- What are the characteristics of companies with strong engagement with your solutions that later became expansion opportunities?
- What actions do you commonly take to improve customer engagement in a way that will lead to future growth?
- How could applying REACH help you expand customer engagement in a more structured and predictable way?

 ACTION PLAN

- Identify two to three customers that demonstrate strong engagement. List what you or your company has done to generate that strong engagement. Define those actions, characteristics, and behaviors.
- Identify two to three customers who you believe have high potential for future growth but don't demonstrate strong engagement with your solution. Define a strategy to improve engagement by applying the concepts you learned in this chapter.
- Score your accounts according to the REACH methodology outlined at the end of the chapter. Identify opportunities to improve your customers' engagement in a way that could increase their willingness to invest more in your products or services.
- Use these activities as input into prioritizing your accounts using the REACH process.

A - Actions

In the REACH Framework™, "Actions" refers to the frequency and relevance of certain events or proactive steps that signal customers' readiness to deepen their investment with you. This component is vital in identifying clues for potential expansion. You will understand how particular events or customer actions contribute to your ability to attract additional investment to your solution.

In this chapter, you will learn:

- What proactive steps customers take that you should be looking for.

- How past increases in spending for your solution can be an indicator of future willingness to invest.

- Why renewal discussions are an excellent time for expansion discussions.

- How you can leverage details from support inquiries and feature requests in your expansion strategy.

- What information you can gather from a customer request to learn more about new features, services, and demos.

- Why encouraging customers to show results from your solution to other internal teams is vital.

For example, a leading provider in health benefits management uncovered a significant growth opportunity when a discussion with one of its clients led to the customer expressing concerns about rising pharmacy claims costs. This expression was precisely the signal the Account Managers were looking for, suggesting the customer's potential interest in exploring the provider's integrated pharmacy cost management solution. This conversation paved the way for additional discussions about how this pharmacy cost management program worked and the benefits it could provide to the customer.

Let's look at how to assess a variety of customer "Actions" effectively.

Recognize Proactive Indicators of Readiness for Growth

A key indicator of a customer's potential for growth lies in their proactive actions regarding your product or service. These actions could manifest in numerous ways. Customers might inquire about advanced features of your product, explore new use cases, add more team members to work with your solution, or even initiate discussions about broadening their use of your offerings.

Additionally, pay attention when your contacts mention other teams or business units that could benefit from your solution. Such mentions often highlight unexplored areas where your product could be highly valuable.

These indicators seem obvious as clues that your client has a potential growth opportunity. However, I cannot tell you how many times I hear about these types of situations from my clients, but when I ask them what steps they took to follow up on these expansion opportunities, there is no response. They could have made a note of these indicators in a system somewhere. They could have told an account executive who was also working with the account. They could have created a sales opportunity in the company's CRM system. But in many cases, there is no concrete follow-up. Really?

For instance, I recently worked with a client that sells real estate technology software. I was facilitating a REACH working session with their Customer Success Managers where I was probing them about a particular client that was using their solution in only two of the client's fifteen office buildings. One of the CSMs mentioned that the customer's internal champion specifically mentioned that a third office building manager was interested in making decisions that my client's data and solution could inform. This type of bright, flashing, green indicator light should blast out that there is an expansion opportunity. Even when you may not be formally responsible for closing the expansion opportunities, you must have a system in place to share this information with whoever is accountable for following up on the expansion sale.

You must start to realize the frequency with which these glaring signals for growth are missed or ignored. Each unaddressed mention of a new use case or an unexplored team's interest represents a missed opportunity or a chance for growth left on the table. These overlooked moments can cumulatively amount to significant revenue loss.

Look for clues that your clients are open to considering additional investment with your company.

I urge you to implement a proactive and systematic approach to prevent these missed opportunities. Start by integrating a process within your team to document and follow up on potential leads or interests expressed by your customers. Use your CRM or Customer Success Platform to its fullest potential, ensuring that every hint of expansion interest is captured and assigned to the right team member for follow-up. Establish regular reviews between your sales and Customer Success team counterparts to discuss these opportunities and plan strategic follow-ups. Remember, the key to capitalizing on growth opportunities is recognizing them and diligently acting upon them.

Look for Patterns of Past Growth and Investment

Evaluating your customers' historical growth in revenue is a valuable predictor of their potential for future expansion. A customer's track record of consistent revenue increases through upselling or cross-selling often indicates their readiness to invest further in your solutions. Such a history suggests customers' satisfaction with your product and an evolving reliance on your solution for meeting their business needs.

Another step is to understand any past patterns in customers' expansion and how these patterns might inform your approach moving forward. Have customers demonstrated a long-term growth pattern over time or are they staying flat? Have they added to investments within existing business teams? Are they growing into different business units? Do they expand their investments only during renewal contract negotiations or have they been open to expanding off-cycle?

To effectively track this information, your data analytics or operations team should regularly review customer revenue trends. They can leverage CRM tools and sales data to clearly depict each customer's financial journey with your product.

This team should be responsible for identifying growth patterns and sharing insights with both the sales and Customer Success teams.

This data can also provide valuable insights into the timing of past investment decisions or highlight which stakeholders were most influential in those decisions. Knowing this history can guide how you best position your solution for future expansion opportunities. By understanding the motivations, timing, and circumstances that led to previous growth in revenue, you can tailor your approach to align with the customer's business trajectory. This proactive approach enables you to anticipate customers' evolving needs and present your solutions in a timely and relevant manner, thus shifting from a reactive to a proactive engagement model.

Another valuable predictor of growth is to look out for customer requests or frustrations that have led to expansion opportunities in the past. Kristen McKenna is the Chief Underwriting Officer and Customer Officer at ParetoHealth, the leading provider of employer-sponsored, self-insured health benefit plans. She understands the subtle art of listening for growth signals in customer conversations and recognizing the patterns. "For us, it's about tuning into the client's pain points," she says. For example, McKenna trains her Account Managers to identify moments when customers express frustration with escalating pharmacy costs or patterns of high-cost claimants.

These are opportunities, McKenna believes, not just for upselling but for genuinely assisting clients to manage their benefits spending more effectively. This type of observation is a mindset of service that often leads to expansion – spotting the chance to introduce ParetoHealth's healthcare cost containment solutions where they can truly make a difference. McKenna asserts, "It's about offering value that aligns perfectly with their needs, and when it does, both parties win." This proactive approach has positioned ParetoHealth as a partner that provides high-value and cost-effective solutions to their member companies.

Evaluate Feedback and Product Request Patterns

Evaluating customers' feedback and product request patterns provides invaluable insights into their potential for expansion. When customers repeatedly inquire about specific features or services, these inquiries often signal a more profound interest or a pressing need beyond how they currently use your product or service. These inquiries reflect an engagement level that may be ripe for expansion, as these questions suggest that customers are exploring ways to derive more value from your offerings but don't know what to do. Such patterns can also highlight areas where your solution could evolve or be better communicated, presenting opportunities to enhance and expand your relationship.

In addition, the nature of these inquiries can be revealing. If customers regularly contact your team about capabilities they should be aware of, it demonstrates a gap in your customers' understanding of the full potential of your product. This gap is an opportunity to educate those customers about existing features and additional solutions your company offers. These interactions create a clear path to discuss how expanding their use of your solutions could meet a broader range of their needs.

Lastly, when customers request additional solutions, it directly points to expansion opportunities. These requests often come from a place of trust and satisfaction with your existing services, implying that they see your company as a solution provider for broader business challenges. By actively listening to these requests and thoughtfully responding, you position your company as a proactive partner in customer success, leading to more productive expansion discussions.

Collaboration with the product management team is essential in evaluating customer feedback and product request patterns. Product managers can provide deep insights into the feasibility of addressing patterns in customer requests and can help prioritize those requests that align with the product roadmap. This ensures that customer feedback directly influences product evolution.

Every few weeks, I run a think tank group where Customer Success leaders, AI vendors, and other AI experts discuss how customer-facing organizations can leverage AI. One of the common use cases that came up early on was how awesome it will be when AI can quickly and easily identify trends and insights from the vast amounts of customer data we receive. As the security of AI solutions expands and companies become more comfortable having their customer feedback and call transcripts available for AI systems to analyze, there is likely to be an explosion of useful information from this data. By the time you are reading this book, these AI solutions may already be available. Take advantage of the power of AI to identify trends among your customers and have AI point out customers who are more likely to be ready for growth opportunities.

Leverage the Dynamics of Renewal Discussions

Understanding the dynamics of renewal discussions is crucial for identifying the timing of expansion opportunities. When customers approach their renewal phase, they're already in a mindset of evaluation and decision-making. This circumstance provides a unique opportunity to reintroduce the value of your solution and propose additional offerings that align with your customers' evolving needs. Renewals are not just administrative checkpoints. Renewals are strategic inflection points where many customers reassess their current solutions and are more receptive to considering enhancements or additional services.

During these discussions, customers are often open to reevaluating their initial decisions and exploring how they can maximize their investment. This openness provides fertile ground for suggesting new solutions to address specific strategic or operational challenges customers may face. It's a time when customers are more likely to consider how expanding their partnership with your company can bring additional benefits, such as improved efficiencies, enhanced features, or better alignment with their long-term goals.

For larger enterprise companies, the renewal period presents a unique opportunity beyond contract continuation. This period may be the only time during the year to secure additional budgets. In big organizations, navigating their complex and political landscape can be difficult, meaning getting off-cycle financial approvals may be challenging. During renewals, decision-makers may be more receptive to exploring expanded solutions. These decision-makers are already engaged in financial discussions and more likely to have access to discretionary funds. This renewal period creates a window where aligning renewal talks and budget availability can facilitate easier approval for expanded investments.

Encourage Customers to Share Results Regularly and Broadly

Your team can encourage your customers to showcase the results and outcomes enabled by your solution. Customers can share their insights (and enthusiasm) at company-wide meetings and functional all-hands presentations. Then, these champions can build their insights into reports and dashboards regularly used by your customers' executive teams.

Sharing can have multiple benefits. First, when customers highlight the successes achieved through your product, these successes not only underscore the value of your solution but also serve as a powerful internal advocacy tool. Sharing creates opportunities for individuals with similar roles or needs to think, "I want to achieve those same results. Tell me more about how you did that." You don't need your customers to discuss your solution specifically (although that may be nice). You want them to talk about the *results* uniquely enabled by using your solution.

Second, you can look for ways to have your solution-enabled outcomes and decisions integrated into reports and dashboards that are used by your executive teams to make decisions. For instance, I work with a client that provides online survey tools that enable businesses to gather insights and feedback from their target audiences. This client strongly encourages its customers to conduct ongoing surveys that deliver results that can be consistently shared with its executive teams. These results are also indicators of company-impacting outcomes, such as measuring their Net Promoter ScoreTM (NPS) scores, Customer Satisfaction (CSAT) scores, or employee engagement scores.

This practice embeds my client's software as an essential part of the company's operational fabric and establishes a vital recurring metric that top executives routinely evaluate. Integrating your solution's data into key executive reports and dashboards creates a scenario where your product becomes synonymous with critical business metrics. This drives a compelling use case for sustained and expanded use of your solution.

This approach not only facilitates customers in quantifying the value gained but also assists them in effectively communicating these results in their internal meetings and forums, enhancing their stature as savvy decision-makers who have brought tangible benefits to their organizations.

EXPANSION ACCELERATOR Encourage your customers to showcase the successful outcomes they get from using your solutions to internal and external stakeholders.

Here are a few additional ways to encourage your customers to display their results.

- Present in all-hands company meetings
- Integrate into executive presentations
- Feature in internal newsletters or communications
- Include in functional or departmental meetings
- Host internal best practice webinars or workshops

- Share results at annual company meetings or sales kickoffs

- Discuss in your fiscal planning sessions and budget review meetings

Score the Quality of Actions as It Relates to the Growth Propensity Index™

As you determine how to score your existing customers to identify their propensity for future growth as well as what you can do to improve that score, here are a few questions to consider.

- What proactive steps has your customer taken that indicate an interest in a deeper investment?

- Does the customer have a history of growing their spending with you?

- Is there an upcoming renewal that creates an opportunity to discuss growth opportunities?

- Has the customer requested information about additional features, licenses, offerings, or services?

- Are there recent strategic initiatives or projects where your solution plays a key role?

- Is your customer sharing results internally with executives, at staff meetings, or all-hands?

Actions - Scoring Methodology

1 - Poor (Minimal or No Proactive Actions)

- There are no requests for additional features, offerings, or services.

- Results and impact are not shared within the customer's organization or with you.

- The customer shows little to no initiative in deepening their investment or exploring broader uses of your solutions.

- There are no recent initiatives or projects where your solution has played a significant role.

- The customer has not demonstrated interest in new strategies or initiatives where your solution could be involved.

- There is no history of the customer increasing their spending or expanding their use of your services.

- There is no upcoming renewal event to serve as an opportunity to discuss expansion.

2 - Fair (Limited Proactive Actions)

- Requests for additional features or services are infrequent.

- Results and impact are rarely shared with internal stakeholders at your customer's company.

- The customer occasionally shows interest in deepening their investment but lacks consistent initiative.

- Your solution has played only a minor role in a few customer initiatives or projects.

- There is limited engagement in discussions about new strategies or initiatives to which your solution could contribute.

- There is a sporadic or minimal history of the customer increasing their spending with your company.

- Upcoming renewals are acknowledged but without significant enthusiasm or planning for growth opportunities.

3 - Good (Moderate Proactive Actions)

- The customer occasionally requests information about additional features.

- Results and impact are regularly shared with internal stakeholders.

- The customer regularly takes steps to deepen their investment, showing interest in more broadly utilizing your solutions.

- Your solution has been involved in several customer initiatives, playing a noticeable role.

- The customer is open to discussions about new strategies where your solution could be beneficial.

- There is a history of occasional increases in spending or expansion in using your solutions.

- Upcoming renewals are seen as opportunities to discuss potential growth, with some proactive engagement.

4 - Very Good (Strong Proactive Actions)

- The customer regularly requests information about new features or services.

- Results and insights are regularly shared and available across the customer's organization.

- The customer frequently initiates actions to deepen their investment and broaden the use of your solutions.

- Your solution is key to many of the customer's initiatives and projects.

- The customer actively seeks to integrate your solution into new strategies and initiatives.

- The customer has a consistent history of increasing their spending and expanding their use of your services.

- Upcoming renewals are actively approached as opportunities for discussing and planning growth.

5 - Excellent (Exceptional Proactive Actions)

- The customer frequently requests advanced features or additional services.

- The customer regularly champions your solution internally at high-level meetings.

- The customer consistently demonstrates a strong initiative to deepen their investment and expand your solution's use.

- Your solution is central to the customer's strategic initiatives and projects, playing a critical role.

- The customer is highly proactive in exploring and implementing new strategies where your solution can add value.

- There is a significant and ongoing increase in the customer's spending and expansion in using your solutions.

- Renewals are strategically used as opportunities for substantial growth discussions and planning.

CHAPTER REVIEW

 QUESTIONS TO CONSIDER

- What actions do your customers take that could indicate their readiness for future growth? What steps do you take to listen for those indicators?
- What data-driven predictors of future growth have you identified? What processes do you use to capture and highlight those indicators?
- What steps can you take to turn around situations where actions or data indicate a customer is not inclined to grow with you?
- How could you use REACH to identify and respond to your customers' actions that could indicate future growth potential or a barrier to growth?

 ACTION PLAN

- Identify two to three actions your customers take or behaviors they demonstrate that could indicate future growth potential. Consider why those actions are strong indicators.
- Identify two to three data-driven predictors of future growth for your business. Consider why those data are strong indicators.
- Work with your data or operations teams to see if there are ways to identify these activities systematically. Always think about ways to prioritize the most important things.
- Score your accounts according to the REACH methodology outlined at the end of this chapter. Identify opportunities to listen more actively to customers' actions that indicate a potential openness to investing more in your products or services.

C – Customer Value

This chapter will discuss the "Customer Value" element of REACH, which focuses on the measurable and intangible benefits customers derive from using your products and services. Understanding and articulating this value is a critical prerequisite to demonstrating how further investment can provide greater returns.

In this chapter, you will learn:

- Why it is essential to quantify the value of your solutions toward achieving customer outcomes.

- How you can understand your customers' goals and how your customers define value.

- How you can identify examples of high-impact outcomes your customers have achieved.

- Why it is crucial to integrate your solution into the business workflow of your client.

- Why it's useful to help customers make the connection between your solution and their goals.

- What value often means to your customers in terms of their personal career progression.

By quantifying the tangible improvements in Key Performance Indicators (KPIs) and aligning your solutions with customer goals, you can establish a starting point for conversations about further investment that would deliver similar results in other parts of your customer's business.

One of my clients in the real estate technology industry makes a solution that helps large companies reduce costs and improve their employee experience by providing data about how office space is utilized. One of this client's customers wanted to decide how to optimize its real estate portfolio and space occupancy. The customer used my client's solution to gather data about how its employees were using its workspace and found that the utilization of one of its buildings was very small after the pandemic. This data gave the customer the confidence to terminate the lease early in one of the buildings and consolidate employees into a nearby office. This enabled millions of dollars in cost avoidance in this one office building and led to discussions about how this customer could expand my client's solution into additional larger buildings.

Why It Is Important to Demonstrate Value from Your Solution

As we dig into the "Customer Value" factor in the REACH Framework™, it's essential to understand why highlighting the value of your solution is pivotal in leading to future expansion opportunities. Articulating this value effectively is not just about presenting data, it's about connecting your solution's impact directly to your customers' strategic goals and desired outcomes. This connection is key to unlocking further investment and fostering a more beneficial relationship. Let's explore why demonstrating this value is helpful and fundamental to your ability to grow revenue from your existing customers.

METRICS THAT MATTER Demonstrate value by connecting your solution's impact to your customers' desired outcomes.

First, quantifying the value of your solution in terms of tangible improvements in your customer's KPIs serves as clear evidence of your solution's effectiveness. When customers can see a direct correlation between the use of your product and improvements in their critical metrics, they are more likely to perceive your solution as an indispensable tool for success. This perception is crucial, especially in a competitive market where customers constantly evaluate the return on their investments.

Second, tying your solution's impact to specific KPIs facilitates more strategic conversations around expansion. Customers are more open to discussing further investment in a solution when they can clearly understand how it contributes to their strategic objectives and goals. For instance, if a customer's KPI is to increase market share and your solution has demonstrably helped in achieving this, positioning additional features or products as logical next steps to support this ongoing goal becomes much easier.

Here are common ways that customers assess the impact and value of a solution.

1. Revenue growth and profitability

2. Operational efficiency

3. Innovation and product development

4. Risk mitigation and compliance

5. Employee engagement and productivity

6. Customer experience and engagement

7. Market expansion and penetration

Understand Your Customer's Desired Outcomes and How They Define Value

A key to demonstrating value is to understand your customers' desired business outcomes and how customers define value in the first place. This understanding requires you to collect specifics of what success looks like for each customer. Every organization has its own set of priorities, challenges, and benchmarks for success. Engaging in thoughtful conversations with your customers is vital, asking probing questions to uncover not just their immediate needs but their long-term goals as well.

Consider the diverse ways different customers might define value. To some, value might be about driving revenue growth or gaining market share. While for others, value could be about operational efficiency, innovation, or customer satisfaction. Recognizing these differences is essential in tailoring your approach. For instance, if you're working with a client in a highly competitive market, they might value rapid innovation and agility. On the other hand, a client in a more mature industry might prioritize cost reduction and operational stability.

Here are a few techniques I use to help my clients capture goals and value targets from their customers.

1. **Leverage the Sales Process:** During initial sales discussions, make it a point to collect detailed information about the customer's goals and expected outcomes. This is the first opportunity to understand what your customer values most and how your solution fits into their business strategy. Ensure this information is passed along to your post-sale teams.

2. **Reaffirm Goals During Implementation:** Use the onboarding or implementation phase as a critical checkpoint to validate and refine the goals collected during the

sales process. This phase often reveals more about the practical aspects of how your solution will be used. It also provides time to more deeply explore how to operationalize your customer's expectations.

3. **Maintain Ongoing Dialogue in Post-Sale Interactions:** Regularly discuss goals and outcomes during routine check-ins or support interactions. This ongoing dialogue ensures that you are always aligned with the customers' current needs and expectations, and these conversations provide an avenue to adjust your approach as their business evolves. Be on the lookout for changes in strategy that may impact how your solution is used. These happen at least once a year during the budget planning cycle.

4. **Validate During Executive Engagement:** When interacting with executives or top-level decision-makers at your customer's organization, continue to discuss and validate the outcomes that are most important to them. Executive insights can provide a broader strategic context to the customer's goals, often highlighting long-term objectives and high-level value definitions.

5. **Look for Changes That Result from Your Customer's Annual Planning Process:** Recognize that business goals and priorities can shift over time. Conduct annual or periodic reviews with your customers to reassess their objectives and how they define value. Most companies revisit their strategies and initiatives at least annually

during their fiscal year planning process. Look for changes that can positively or negatively impact how customers measure value from your solution.

Amy Elrod is the VP of Customer Success at Docebo, the leading customer and employee learning platform for global enterprises. Elrod works with her team to develop and strengthen skills to understand value and spot opportunities for customer growth. She says, "CSMs can become more adept at uncovering these chances for growth as they expand their business savvy and their maturity working with customer. They become better at connecting the dots across their customer interactions to identify ways their customers can get more value from our solutions."

Elrod's approach includes continuous coaching and using tools like Gong's call reviews to elevate her team's skills. She emphasizes the power of recognizing the "easy wins" like when a customer defines value in a way that aligns perfectly with Docebo's offerings. This enables her team of CSMs to be viewed by customers as strategic partners, while also contributing to Docebo's top-line revenue growth.

Remember, value is not a one-size-fits-all concept. I encourage my clients to continuously engage with their customers to understand and adapt to their customers' changing needs and definitions of value. By staying in tune with customers' evolving journey, you can be ready to demonstrate how their expanded use of your products or solutions can contribute to them achieving their future strategic goals.

Quantify the Impact on Customer Outcomes

I recently worked with a client who provides a no-code marketing campaign creation solution for global brands. Together, we developed a Return on Investment (ROI) calculator that enabled his Customer Success Managers and his Account Managers to quantify the savings their customers were achieving by using their solution. For example, they had a large customer paying hundreds of dollars per hour to digital marketing agencies for the type of marketing programs the customer's internal marketers could now create with my client's solution for a tiny fraction of the cost. This value calculator we designed enabled my client's CSMs to demonstrate how much their customer could save on digital marketing agency costs by expanding the solution to other business units and regions.

One objection I often hear from my clients when we discuss measuring ROI is that their customers won't share all the information they need to calculate the ROI. You can often solve this problem by making estimates and letting your customers correct the data to add precision. Your customers want to be able to show the value of their work too. These calculations make them look good to their internal stakeholders.

METRICS THAT MATTER
If your customers won't share the data you need to calculate ROI, start with your best-guess estimates.

Let me go back to the story we just discussed. Calculating the savings of using my client's solution compared to hiring an outside agency requires knowing the hourly cost of the agency and the number of hours it takes to complete an email. The client might not be willing to share the hourly rate or how many hours it takes the agency to create and build the email into their marketing campaign (or in this case, they might be too embarrassed to say how much it costs!).

However, since my client works with hundreds of customers and may be familiar with benchmarks for agency costs, we might start with an estimate that the agency charges $250 per hour and that the typical email campaign takes 40 hours to complete from start to finish. This gives you a cost of $10,000 per email. When my client shared this value calculation with the customer, the customer said, "No, no, no. It is more like $235 per hour, and it takes 60 hours." The client was willing to confirm data to make the estimate more precise even when they weren't ready to share the data explicitly. Try this approach with your customers. You may be surprised.

Integrate Your Solution into the Business Workflow

A key aspect of demonstrating value is how your solution is woven into your customer's workflows and operations. This is important for a few reasons.

First, this integration into their workflow signifies that your product transcends being merely an additional tool. Your solution is an essential component of customers' daily business functions. This dependence ensures that your solution is not seen as peripheral or optional but as a fundamental part of their operational framework. When your product is seamlessly embedded into customers' workflows, this integration enables smoother processes, enhances efficiency, and becomes indispensable for the ongoing operations of their business. This level of integration fosters reliance on your solution, making it less likely for the customer to consider alternatives and more likely to expand your solution's usage.

Second, such integration is a strong indicator of customer commitment and satisfaction. The integration reflects your customers' recognition of your solution's value to their business, leading to a deeper, more strategic partnership. This alignment with their business processes and goals strengthens the relationship and opens avenues for further exploration of how your solution can support new initiatives or address challenges they face. An integrated solution becomes a part of your customers' success story, making your product a key player in their growth and evolution.

This creates a great opportunity for Customer Success and Account Management teams to work collaboratively with the product teams. Together, they can ensure that any new solutions are not just a bundle of added features but become useful components of the customer's daily operations. By working together, these teams can ensure that product enhancements and roadmaps are closely aligned with the evolving needs of customers, leading to increased opportunities for expansion.

Understand Your Solution's Impact on Your Stakeholders' Career Progression and Aspirations

An often overlooked yet critical aspect that can significantly influence expansion opportunities is the personal stake or professional aspirations of essential stakeholders within your customer's organization. Consider how the success of your solution adds value to the career development, ambitions, or promotion trajectory of individual stakeholders, such as your power-users, your internal champions, or your executive sponsors.

Imagine a scenario where a power-user of your product or service at one of your customer's organizations is an ambitious manager aiming for an expanded leadership role. By successfully implementing and increasing the use of your solution, that ambitious manager would directly contribute to the company's business outcomes and operational efficiency. She might have a personal motivation to communicate internally to company executives and functional leaders in other business units about the outcomes your solution delivered. She might aspire that different business units could adopt and benefit from the same solution she brought into the company and made successful.

Understanding and acknowledging the value of your solution in personal motivation can be a powerful tool in driving expansion. When a solution meets organizational goals and aligns with key stakeholders' private interests, this nexus creates a unique and compelling reason for them to advocate for broader adoption.

To drive expansion opportunities, emphasize how your solution's success can accelerate your stakeholder's career trajectory.

Score the Quality of Customer Value as It Relates to the Growth Propensity Index™

As you determine how to score your existing customers to identify their propensity for future growth as well as what you can do to improve that score, here are a few questions to consider.

- How does your customer measure the value of your solution to the business?

- What metrics or KPIs have improved because of using your solution? Are the results impactful?

- How has your solution contributed to the customer achieving their business goals?

- Can you identify examples of high-impact outcomes your customer has achieved?

- How does the value your customer achieves compare to their investment in your solution?

Customer Value - Scoring Methodology

1 - Poor (Minimal Recognition of Value)

- The customer shows little to no recognition of the value received from your solutions.

- There are no clear metrics or KPIs that have improved as a result of using your product.

- There is minimal or no evidence that your solution contributes to the customer's strategic goals.

- High-impact outcomes or significant improvements attributable to your solutions are not identified or acknowledged by the customer.

2 - Fair (Limited Recognition of Value)

- The customer has a limited understanding or appreciation of the value provided by your solutions.

- A few metrics or KPIs show slight improvement, but the connection to your product is not firmly established.

- Your solution's contribution to the customer's achievement of strategic goals is recognized but not fully leveraged or understood.

- Examples of positive outcomes from using your solutions are limited and are not prominently highlighted by the customer.

3 - Good (Moderate Recognition of Value)

- The customer acknowledges the value received from your solutions, but there may be room for greater recognition.

- Several metrics or KPIs show improvement, and the customer attributes some of this progress to your product.

- The customer sees your solution as contributing to their strategic goals, but the full potential may not be realized.

- The customer can identify specific examples where your solution has led to positive outcomes, though these examples may not be consistently highlighted.

4 - Very Good (Strong Recognition of Value)

- The customer clearly recognizes and appreciates the value delivered by your solutions.

- Multiple metrics or KPIs have significantly improved, and the customer attributes this success to your product.

- Your solution is seen as a key contributor to achieving the customer's strategic goals.

- The customer frequently cites examples of high-impact outcomes achieved through the use of your solution, showcasing your solution's value.

5 - Excellent (Exceptional Recognition of Value)

- The customer consistently and enthusiastically recognizes the strong value delivered by your solutions.

- A wide range of metrics or KPIs show substantial improvement directly linked to the use of your solutions.

- The customer views your solutions as integral to their strategic success, with clear and measurable contributions.

- Numerous examples of significant, high-impact outcomes achieved with your solutions are regularly highlighted and celebrated by the customer.

CHAPTER REVIEW

 QUESTIONS TO CONSIDER

- Why is it important to quantify the value your customers receive from using your products or services? Why is this essential if you want to grow your future business with that customer?
- How do your customers define value? How do you learn how your customers determine the value of using your solutions?
- How do you quantify the value of your solution to your customers? Do they understand how you measure your value and find those metrics helpful?
- How can you demonstrate how your solutions add value to your customers' business outcomes? How can you quantify the impact?
- How could REACH help show value to your customers in a way that increases their propensity to grow their investment with your business?

 ACTION PLAN

- Identify three to five ways your solutions measurably contribute to how your customers achieve their intended business outcomes.
- Identify how you can quantify the value of your solutions. Define the inputs or assumptions you need to capture. Consider ways to estimate or collect that information.
- Identify two to three customers who are receiving substantial value from your solutions. Consider ways for those customers to share their results with other business groups, regions, or peers.
- Score your accounts according to the REACH methodology outlined at the end of the chapter. Identify opportunities to measure and communicate the value of your solutions.

H – Horizons

The Horizons Factor helps you assess the growth opportunities "on the horizon" that may be reflected in a customer's longer-term strategic objectives, financial goals, or competitive initiatives and results. This factor is about understanding and anticipating the alignment of your solutions to the future growth opportunities within your customers' organization. Getting to the heart of this opportunity goes beyond your customers' immediate needs and looks at the broader picture, considering the presence of new business units, geographical regions, or through organizational changes like mergers and acquisitions. The Horizons Factor also assesses whether your customers' financial condition and strategic direction would be consistent with a propensity to expand their relationship with you.

In this chapter, you will learn:

- How to assess the potential to expand into new business units and regions.

- How upcoming strategic, financial, or organizational changes impact growth opportunities.

- What actions to take if your customers are engaged in mergers, acquisitions, and expansions.

- How to interpret your customer's financial health when considering expansion potential.

- How to capitalize on Mergers and Acquisitions as growth opportunities.

 AI will make it easier to learn about important characteristics of your accounts related to their strategic goals, financial performance, and organizational structure.

Encourage Expansion into New Business Units and Regions

One of the most apparent and fertile grounds for uncovering new expansion opportunities lies within the landscape of a company's diverse brands, business units, and geographies. This diversity certainly presents opportunities for future potential growth. When you can successfully navigate the complexities of introducing your solutions across various segments of a larger organization, you expand your revenue potential and solidify your position as a critical business partner.

The value of this approach lies in its ability to tap into previously unserved or underserved areas of your customer's business. By reaching different business units and geographic regions, you diversify your revenue stream and reduce dependency on a single business unit's performance.

However, this path is often riddled with unique challenges that can make this business development process more complex than it initially appears. One challenge is when different business units or regional divisions operate independently. Each unit or division may have its own decision-making processes, budgetary constraints, and business priorities. What works in one business unit might not work in a different business unit. Sometimes, leaders even prefer to take a different path to highlight their units' independence.

Another challenge is that some large organizations have internal dynamics that can be difficult to understand from the outside. Business units may operate in silos and be guarded by gatekeepers who are cautious about external influences, including solutions from other units within the same company. Breaking through these barriers can require tactfully navigating your customer's internal politics, building relationships, and earning trust across different organization segments.

A third challenge is that these business units and regions may have varied requirements and pain points. A solution that addresses the needs of the North American market might not be a good fit for Asia-Pacific or Europe. Factors such as language barriers, cultural differences, regulatory issues, and time zone discrepancies may complicate expansion communication and efforts.

One of the most significant hurdles my clients face when trying to expand into new business units or regions is developing strong internal champions. Without advocates who understand your solutions' value and are willing to effectively vouch for those solutions internally, penetrating these new segments can be daunting. Two of the most important outcomes that Customer Success Managers and Account Managers can contribute to are building these relationships and delivering undeniable value that their advocates can champion across the company.

EXPANSION ACCELERATOR: Develop strong advocates who will vouch for your solution to other business units and regions.

Maximize the Strategic Alignment to Long-Term Customer Goals

Aligning your solutions with your customer's long-term strategic objectives is imperative when fostering expansion within your customer accounts. This alignment helps transform your role from a vendor into a strategic partner, creating a faster path for future expansion opportunities. Are there aspects of your solution that have been integral to your customers' strategic long-term initiatives or significant projects? This alignment strongly indicates your customers' perceived value and potential to seek deeper engagement.

For Customer Success Managers and Account Managers, achieving this strategic alignment involves actively listening during interactions to pick up on clues about future projects, growth areas, and potential challenges the customer anticipates in the future. Once you understand your customer's strategic goals, you need to clearly articulate how your solutions align with and can support these objectives. The objective is to establish your solution as useful for today and an integral part of your customer's future success.

Take the example of a healthcare technology company integrating a learning management system (LMS) to streamline its customer training process. This decision to upgrade the LMS aligned with a company-wide strategic initiative to improve profitability while delivering great experiences to its customers. This alignment has implications for future expansion. As the solution proves its value for customer-facing training, the solution will naturally open doors for broader application within the organization.

Once the team can demonstrate that this new LMS effectively reduces customer training costs while boosting productivity, expanding the use of the LMS to the human resources organization will be a logical progression because human resources can potentially use the LMS as a platform for employee, compliance, and new-hire training. Expanding the use of this LMS aligns very well with the company's approach to improving profitability while delivering great experiences.

Assess the Company's Size, Financial Considerations, and Growth Outlook

When evaluating a customer's potential for growth, it's essential to consider the customer's size, financial strength, and growth trajectory. These factors can significantly influence your customers' capacity and willingness to expand their relationship with your solution. Larger organizations often have more resources, bigger budgets, and a broader scope for implementation, making them prime candidates for expansion. However, your customers' size can also mean more complex decision-making processes and longer sales cycles. Understanding the nuances of navigating these larger entities is crucial to effectively tap into their growth potential.

METRICS THAT MATTER
When evaluating a customer's potential for growth, consider their size, financial strength, and growth trajectory.

Conversely, with smaller customers, there may be a realization that your company has reached the maximum share of your customers' available spending, or "share of wallet," which is the proportion of a customer's total expenditures that is spent on your company's products or services. This metric is critical as it helps gauge how much more of your customers' spending could potentially be captured with your solutions.

Increasing your "share of wallet" contributes to driving expansion revenue. Strategically, the REACH Framework™ guides Customer Success and Account Managers to not only preserve but also expand this share by continuously identifying and acting upon up-sell and cross-sell opportunities that align with customer needs.

Financial strength is another important indicator. A financially healthy customer with steady revenue growth, good profit margins, and a solid, competitive position is generally more open to considering expansion opportunities. Leaders at financially strong companies may also feel less stress in the budgeting process and additional investment resources may be available to fund projects with strong ROI and benefits. Companies in a strong financial position are often more open to exploring other technologies and solutions that promise to enhance their competitive edge.

Conversely, a company facing financial challenges might be less inclined or able to pursue expansion opportunities. These indicators might be apparent as declining revenues, layoffs, or poor market performance. In these situations, the focus of Customer Success Managers and Account Managers should shift toward supporting these clients through their tough times, maintaining solid relationships, and maintaining trust so that you can revisit these opportunities once the company regains its footing.

Last, a company's growth trajectory – whether rapidly expanding, stable, or in a consolidation phase – can help you anticipate its approach to new investments. Rapidly growing companies might look for solutions that can scale with their growth, presenting good expansion opportunities even when value recognition is delayed. On the other hand, companies in a stable or consolidation phase might focus more on optimizing current operations and limiting investment in additional solutions that don't bring immediate returns. Tailoring your approach to align with your customers' current growth phase is vital to unlocking potential expansion opportunities with these customers.

Consider Mergers and Acquisitions as Growth Opportunities

Mergers and acquisitions (M&A) can present unique and significant opportunities for driving expanded investment in your business. M&As can substantially change organizational structure, priorities, and strategies. When an existing customer is involved in M&A activities, either as the acquired or the acquirer, that situation is the perfect time to assess how your account growth strategies fit into this new business reality.

If your customer acquires a new company, the acquisition presents a prime opportunity for your solutions to become the standard during the corporate integration. Many acquirers seek ways to consolidate vendors, simplify the contracting process, and gain efficiency from best practices. You must quickly identify the acquired company's existing solutions and articulate how your solutions can provide added value and a smooth integration process.

On the flip side, if your customer is acquired, this situation opens a path to introduce your solution to a broader audience within the acquiring company. In this situation, you should look for ways to demonstrate your solution's value to the acquiring entity and how much additional value your solution could provide to the broader organization.

If your customer is acquired, take the opportunity to introduce your solution to the acquiring company.

In both situations, being proactive and persistent is key. Actively seeking information about any M&A as early as possible and establishing contact with key stakeholders in both the acquiring and acquired companies can provide valuable insights and opportunities to advocate for your solutions and influence critical decision-makers. As a CSM or Account Manager, you may have such a strong relationship with your customer contacts that they share valuable information with you that will help you better understand the situation.

Remember my client who makes software for the car dealership industry? One of that client's single-store accounts was acquired by a larger company with over 60 locations that used a competitor's software product. Once my client heard about the acquisition, the team sprang into action.

The general manager of this one dealership was a vocal advocate, urging the new owners to move the rest of the 60 locations to my client's software platform. Over the next few months, the bigger company did just that. My client had no growth opportunity when it was just the original one-store dealership. But once that one store became part of a bigger dealership group, the growth potential exploded.

Score the Quality of Customer Value as It Relates to the Growth Propensity Index™

As you determine how to score your existing customers to identify their propensity for future growth as well as what you can do to improve that score, here are a few questions to consider.

- Are there new business units or regions that could benefit from your solution?

- How do recent or upcoming strategic, financial, or organizational changes impact growth opportunities?

- Are there additional use cases where your solutions could help your customer achieve more value?

- Are there mergers, acquisitions, or expansions planned that could create a new need for your solution?

- Is there a budget available for any expansion investment?

- Is there a significant opportunity to capture a higher "share of wallet"?

Horizons – Scoring Methodology

1 - Poor (Limited Growth Horizon)

- No new business units or regions where your solutions could be beneficial have been identified.

- Recent or upcoming strategic, financial, or organizational changes are not expected to create new opportunities.

- There are no additional use cases identified where your products could add value.

- The customer has no plans for mergers, acquisitions, or expansions that could necessitate your solutions.

- There is no budget for expansion or compelling events driving growth opportunities.

2 - Fair (Some Growth Horizon)

- Few new business units or regions exist that could be identified as potential areas for your solutions.

- Some strategic, financial, or organizational changes may slightly impact growth opportunities.

- A limited number of additional use cases for your products have been identified.

- There are periodic plans for mergers, acquisitions, or expansions that could lead to new needs for your solutions.

- A limited budget is available for expansion, with few compelling events to drive growth opportunities.

3 - Good (Moderate Growth Horizon)

- Several new business units or regions where your solutions could be applied have been identified.

- Upcoming strategic, financial, or organizational changes will likely create future growth opportunities.

- Multiple additional use cases for your products or services have been identified.

- The customer has potential plans for mergers, acquisitions, or expansions that could create new needs for your solutions.

- A moderate budget is available for expansion, with some compelling events indicating potential growth opportunities.

4 - Very Good (Strong Growth Horizon)

- Numerous new business units or regions have been identified as promising areas for your solutions.

- Significant strategic, financial, or organizational changes will create substantial growth opportunities.

- Your products or services could provide significant value in many additional use cases.

- The customer has active plans for mergers, acquisitions, or expansions that will likely necessitate your solutions.

- A considerable budget is allocated for expansion, with several compelling events driving growth opportunities.

5 - Excellent (Exceptional Growth Horizon)

- Many new business units or regions have been identified as fertile ground for your solutions.

- Significant strategic, financial, or organizational changes are poised to create extensive growth opportunities.

- Your products or services have numerous potential additional use cases that can deliver exceptional value.

- The customer has ongoing plans for mergers, acquisitions, or expansions, creating a high demand for your solutions.

- A significant budget is available for expansion, with compelling events driving substantial growth opportunities.

CHAPTER REVIEW

 QUESTIONS TO CONSIDER

- What business characteristics do your customers demonstrate that indicate they are most likely to grow their investment with you? What do you observe from your existing customers that have grown with you?
- Do your high-potential customers have multiple business units? Do they operate in different regions? Do they have specific numbers of employees? What is the size of their revenue? What are other considerations?
- How do these characteristics impact their willingness to grow with you?
- How do you learn about the strategic initiatives, financial situation, and organizational changes that make your customers more or less likely to expand their investment?
- How can you and your team apply REACH to help you more consistently and predictably identify a customer's propensity to grow based on the Horizons Factor?

 ACTION PLAN

- Identify three to five customers with characteristics based on the Horizons Factor that make them strong candidates for future growth. Note the common themes and insights.
- Identify three to five customers where you have difficulty identifying a situation in which these customers have potential for high growth. Note the common themes and insights.
- Score your accounts according to the definitions outlined in this chapter. When evaluating the most predictive characteristics, consider the takeaways from your observations.
- Use this plan as input into prioritizing your accounts using the REACH process.

Part 3

Putting REACH into Action

Accelerate Your Expansion Growth with REACH

You have learned about how REACH can help your organization accelerate expansion growth from your existing customer base. You have reviewed the five strategic factors needed to increase the customer's propensity to invest with you. You have read about companies like yours using these processes to improve their business results.

You may have also wondered how to apply this framework and these processes to your business. I hope this book will inspire you to act, particularly now that you have a well-organized strategic framework designed explicitly for Customer Success and Account Management teams.

This chapter presents a roadmap to operationalize REACH in your business. You will see the steps necessary to add rigor and structure, so you can feel more confident about your team's ability to achieve its expansion targets.

In my consulting business, I work closely with my clients to implement this approach. They appreciate the fact that I have worked with many companies struggling with similar challenges. My past experience enables us to make efficient progress, avoid common pitfalls, and tailor the best solution for their company, employees, and customers. You can work through these steps yourself or you can call me to help you design and implement this process.

Introduce Your Team to REACH with a Training Workshop

When I kick off this journey with my clients, I prefer to start with a training workshop conducted either on-site or remotely. The workshop creates an opportunity for my clients to realize how they can benefit from applying REACH, learn about the methodology, and practice many of the skills and techniques in a series of role-playing scenarios.

In exercises where we simulate real customer situations, CSMs and Account Managers learn to understand the concepts through practical application, enabling them to get a feel for their effectiveness. These practice conversations also create an opportunity to learn best practices from each other. One of my favorite activities is demonstrating the value of active listening and asking probing questions.

During this training workshop, we also discuss how best to track each customer's current status and monitor progress

PROCESS FLOW TO APPLY REACH IN YOUR BUSINESS

TRAIN
Your Team on REACH

▼

EVALUATE
Expansion Readiness

▼

PRIORITIZE
Accounts by Growth Propensity

▼

UNCOVER
Expansion Opportunities

▼

DEVELOP
Your Account Expansion Plan

▼

DRIVE
Expansion Efforts and Nurture Accounts

▼

EXECUTE
Your Close Plan

▼

MEASURE
Results and Refine Strategies

against actions needed to increase the customer's propensity to grow with you in the future. This will be important when you later build these steps into your operational systems and software platforms.

Assess Your Existing Accounts Using the REACH Framework™

The next step is to get a list of your existing accounts and assess them through the five factors in REACH: Relationships, Engagement, Actions, Customer Value, and Horizons. Ideally, the scoring system provides a structured approach to evaluating and rating each account, but this process isn't about just assigning a score. Understanding the "why" behind each score is equally as important as assigning that score. This process also allows you to think about what you can do more or less of to increase the customer's score and propensity to grow with you in the future.

Before rolling out the REACH Framework™ across all your accounts, starting small is better. Have your CSMs or Account Managers score a manageable number of customers – perhaps five to ten each – and then come together to review the results. This initial evaluation helps ensure the scoring reflects expected patterns and provides a chance to refine the approach before assessing your entire customer base. Through this process, your teams can calibrate their understanding of each factor, ensuring consistency and accuracy in the broader application of REACH.

Documenting the strengths and opportunities for each of the five factors is critical. These notes will ultimately provide input later for creating tailored expansion strategies for each customer. This documentation also helps you track progress and changes over time so you can continuously improve and adjust the effectiveness of your strategy. For accounts that don't score highly on a particular factor, identifying actionable steps to take for improving that score can be helpful.

Update and Configure Your CRM or Customer Success Platform for REACH

While some of my clients track results in a spreadsheet, many prefer to summarize information about their customers in their CRM system or Customer Success Platform. I am currently talking to several platform providers about building out an object in their solution that tracks the status of customers according to REACH. At the very least, each factor should have a dedicated space for scoring and capturing detailed notes explaining the rationale behind each score and the action items to improve.

You can also build these REACH Factors into your solution directly. For example, you can create a simple custom object in Salesforce that provides a field to capture the score of each factor along with relevant notes and action items for each one. Several Customer Success Platform providers like Gainsight, ChurnZero, Catalyst, Client Success, and Totango allow you to build tailored fields to capture this type of information. These fields can also be synced to your CRM system, so they become visible to other teams across your company. Having REACH data in your daily workflow makes you much more likely to use it. Capturing the information this way provides easy visibility, consistency in scoring, and scalability. Having the data at your fingertips also simplifies

REACH DOCUMENTATION IN SALESFORCE CRM

Salesforce — Home | Accounts | Contacts | Sales ˅ | Service ˅ | Marketing ˅ | Calendar | Dashboards

˅ REACH

Relationships ℹ
Very strong relationship with CEO Pierce and CCO Brendan. Brendan has been a strong advocate internally and with the board. Relationship goes back almost 2 yrs. Hosted his team at an event last year. New VP of CS Stephanie just started. She used our solution in her previous company. I plan to meet in person over the next 3 months.

Relationships Score
5

Engagement ℹ
Our solution is mission critical for their marketers. Used every day with strong adoption of core features. Their partners have also been using it. Started pilot of our just released AI features. Expect to roll it out broadly in next 2 months. They are showing results delivered through use of our product at their Revenue Kickoff in February.

Engagement Score
5

Actions ℹ
EMEA region leaders recently requested a demo of our AI features. Their license renewal is coming in June, which creates an opportunity for expansion. They tend to increase their license usage each year.

Actions Score
4

Customer Value ℹ
They can quantify the value of our solution and are seeing 5X return on their costs. Our solution saves them from having to do manual work, points out recommendations, and helps them save significantly on marketing agency costs. Showed results with our value calculator.

Customer Value Score
4

Horizons ℹ
EMEA region is growing quickly. They also recently acquired a smaller company and are considering rolling us out there once the transition is finished. They expect to hire 10 new users in the next 12 months.

Horizons Score
5

Growth Propensity Index ℹ
4.6

reporting so leadership can easily see which customers fall into the high-potential or low-potential categories and why. This reporting also enables leadership to track the actions you are taking to nurture and develop these expansion opportunities.

There is exciting future potential to use AI and predictive analytics to improve the impact of REACH. These AI-enabled capabilities could eventually be used to automatically evaluate and update the Growth Propensity Index™ of each account. This would generate an enormous leap in efficiency and accuracy – and uncover hidden opportunities – allowing your team to focus even more on strategy and driving these expansion opportunities.

Prioritize Your Accounts for Growth Potential

Next up is to prioritize and categorize your accounts based on their potential for growth. Just like how marketing teams use lead scoring to help sales teams identify and prioritize the most promising leads, you can use REACH to segment and prioritize your accounts. For example, you can group accounts into categories of high, moderate, and low potential for growth, then define the appropriate strategy for customers in each category.

The primary method I use for prioritizing accounts is the Growth Propensity Index™ aggregated score based on how each account is evaluated against the five REACH Factors.

This framework provides a quantitative measure to gauge the likelihood of each customer account being a strong candidate for expansion opportunities. Remember that the GPI isn't intended to be perfect. It adds structure, rigor, and data to what I often see among my clients as "finger in the wind" assessments of which accounts to pursue.

 The Growth Propensity Index™ does not need to be perfect. It adds structure, rigor, and data to what is often a squishy process.

Grouping accounts for targeted strategies:

1. **High Potential for Growth:** These accounts exhibit strong scores across most, if not all, REACH Factors. These customers should be your primary focus as they present the most significant expansion opportunities. Consider developing customized strategies and dedicating more time and resources to grow these accounts.

2. **Moderate Potential for Growth:** Accounts in this category show promise in some REACH Factors but may need improvement in others. These accounts may require nurturing and targeted engagement to move them into the high-potential category. These accounts may benefit from specific initiatives to enhance one or more REACH Factors, such as strengthening relationships, increasing product engagement, or delivering value.

3. **Low Potential for Growth:** These accounts score low in several REACH Factors, indicating limited immediate opportunities for expansion. Your strategy here might be to maintain the current level of investment and engagement and monitor for any changes that might increase those accounts' potential. Your time and efforts to

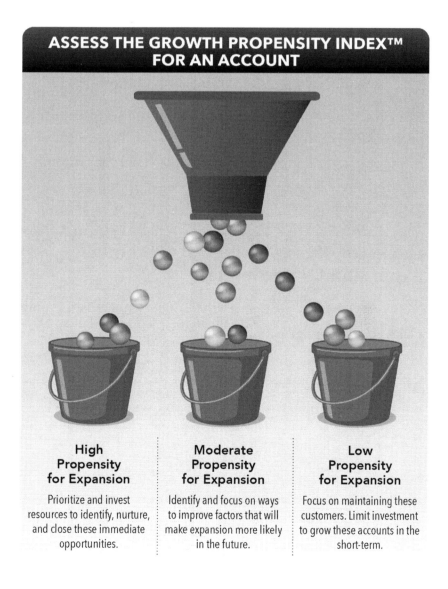

expand investments are better allocated to accounts with higher growth potential. This group of customers could be targeted for digital campaigns, email nurturing, and one-to-many efforts.

Having many accounts with low or moderate growth potential is okay. The critical thing is that you have now identified and segmented them so your company can develop a thoughtful, strategic approach for managing resources effectively while fostering potential opportunities. Although not currently primed for significant expansion, these accounts still hold value and can benefit from a tailored yet scalable approach. Refer to the strategies in previous chapters for ideas about how to improve the likelihood that these customers can become larger growth opportunities in the future.

Listen for Clues and Identify Potential Expansion Opportunities

Now that you are attuned to specific characteristics that make customers strong candidates for expanding their relationships, you can start listening more closely during your interactions with these customers for expansion opportunities. This is an important skill to improve and demonstrate in your daily work.

I run workshops where we practice integrating different questioning and listening techniques into customer discussions. This process helps Customer Success Managers and

Account Managers develop conversational questions designed to subtly but effectively uncover clues for potential expansion opportunities. These questions are not meant to be an interrogation or an interview. They are intended to flow naturally within regular interactions such as one-on-ones, cadence calls, customer on-site visits, or business reviews.

EXPANSION ACCELERATOR Your teams should practice listening for clues in training workshops where they can role play and become more comfortable with these new skills.

In these ongoing conversations, CSMs and Account Managers can discover valuable insights that help identify growth opportunities and how additional investment in their companies' products and services might benefit your clients. You can also learn about potential barriers to expansion that might need to be overcome, such as resource constraints, budget limitations, incumbent contracts, or strategy shifts.

On the next page, you'll find a few examples that I use with my clients to demonstrate how they can more effectively listen, learn, and uncover clues that lead to the identification of future expansion opportunities.

Using these active listening and probing skills can shift the mindset of many teams. Asking questions is a sign of engagement and curiosity. And asking questions demonstrates that you are trying to understand your customers more deeply so that you can better serve them. Think of each interaction with your customers as an opportunity to have a strategic conversation and partner with them for mutual growth.

SAMPLE QUESTIONS TO UNCOVER CLUES FOR POTENTIAL EXPANSION

Technique	Description	Examples of Questions to Ask
Ask Open Ended Questions	These are questions that cannot be answered with a simple yes or no, prompting a more detailed response.	"What other teams at your company are doing [insert your topic]? How do you interact with your peers in those organizations? How do you share best practices?"
Ask Probing Questions	Delve deeper into a subject by asking questions that require further explanation and reflection.	"How do those other teams you mentioned work similarly to your team? What different tools or methods do they use? What stands out about their processes?"
Demonstrate Active Listening	Engage attentively with the speaker by acknowledging, providing feedback, and summarizing their points to show understanding and that their message is being fully received and considered.	"It seems quite challenging to coordinate and share best practices when each team has its own system. You said that creates silos. Tell me more about that."
Ask Diagnostic Questions	Pose inquiries aimed at discovering the root cause of a problem to understand the underlying issues before proposing solutions.	"Considering the variety of tools used across teams for [insert your benefit], can you walk me through any specific challenges this has created? For instance, how does this impact the overall efficiency and productivity of your [insert outcomes]?"

Develop an Account Plan for Expansion Growth

The next step to apply the REACH Framework™ is to share the insights with your stakeholders and develop an Account Expansion Plan. This stage translates the information you have been gathering, your observations from your REACH scoring, and any other data analytics input into actionable strategies tailored to each customer's situation.

This account plan is a blueprint that outlines the steps and strategies necessary to grow the accounts for CSMs or Account Managers who have full accountability for expanding the relationships. This plan also can be a resource used by CSMs and Account Managers when discussing an account with their sales account executive counterpart.

Account Expansion Plans commonly include the following elements.

1. Identified white space or expansion opportunities based on the insights gathered

2. Stakeholder mapping to identify and engage key decision-makers and influencers

3. Actionable goals with specific milestones to track progress

4. The resource allocation needs required to achieve the goals

5. Roles and responsibilities for you and your colleagues

6. Risk assessment of the potential challenges with proposed plans to address those challenges

Collaboration is critical for CSMs or Account Managers who share accountability for expansion with a sales account executive. My most successful clients have developed processes where the CSMs, Account Managers, and Sales Account Executives regularly pool their insights to create a unified Account Expansion Plan. This deep collaboration ensures that both parties are aligned and that the account plan leverages the strengths and insights of your company's relevant team members.

Occasionally, this step involves "passing along the opportunity" to the sales rep or creating an opportunity in a CRM system like Salesforce. Sometimes, this opportunity is referred to as a "Customer Success Qualified Lead." Just like it is valuable for a sales team to provide detailed handoff information to the implementation team after a sale is closed, it is just as beneficial for CSMs or Account Managers to offer similarly detailed handoff information so the sales rep can move the opportunity forward.

EXPANSION ACCELERATOR Growing relationships with existing clients is a team sport. Share learnings and insights regularly across CSMs, Account Managers, and Sales.

This handoff could include creating detailed documentation, conducting internal expansion opportunity handoff calls, or making warm introductions to key stakeholders at the customer's organization. Having the REACH Score with details behind the score provides powerful insights that will help sales if they are accountable for closing these opportunities.

Engage with the Customer to Unlock Expansion Opportunities and Address Concerns

You are now ready to engage with the customer about these potential expansion opportunities. However, rather than fishing around for possible opportunities, your approach can be highly targeted and purposeful.

Ideally, you can integrate the early stages of your discovery and expansion process into your ongoing engagement with your customers. The goal is to create an open dialogue where expansion opportunities are explored as a natural progression of the existing partnership. You also want to ensure the customer doesn't feel pressured or defensive.

In these strategic customer conversations, you hope to discuss the identified expansion opportunities and get the customer's perspective. You also want to uncover and address any concerns the customer may have or barriers they face regarding expansion. As the dialogue progresses, you want to agree on the next steps, which could be a more detailed discussion, a proposal presentation, or a follow-up meeting with additional team members who need to be involved.

Optimize Your Process with an Expansion Close Plan

Having an Expansion Close Plan for your expansion opportunity adds rigor, predictability, and efficiency to your process. Just like Sales Account Executives working with prospects often leverage a close plan to get their sales deal across the line, you can use a similar approach.

Recall that the Expansion Close Plan outlines key actions, timelines, and milestones to move from identifying an expansion opportunity to successfully closing the deal. Unlike the sales close plans for new prospects, this close plan is customized for an expansion situation.

A good Expansion Close Plan outlines steps, including the following elements.

1. Opportunity assessment

2. Proposal creation and presentation

3. Identification and resolution of challenges and barriers

4. Negotiation and revisions

5. Finalizing and contracting

6. Implementation plan

You can download an example of an Expansion Close Plan at www.rodcherkas.com/resources, or contact me on LinkedIn if you want to work together.

Track and Measure Your Results

To ensure the effectiveness of your expansion strategies, you will want to track and report on your forecasts and results. When I work with clients, I recommend building these into an Expansion Impact Dashboard. This dashboard can include reports and visualizations related to the elements.

- List of customer accounts prioritized by their Growth Propensity Index™
- Segmentation of accounts with High, Medium, and Low propensity to expand
- REACH scoring and notes for customer accounts
- Pipeline and forecast of open expansion opportunities
- List of closed-won expansion opportunities
- Links to Expansion Close Plans for open expansion opportunities
- Links to account plans for high-potential expansion accounts

Regularly update your Expansion Impact Dashboard with the latest quantitative and qualitative data to maintain the dashboard's relevance. Schedule periodic reviews with key stakeholders to discuss insights, learnings, and actions derived from your efforts. Also ensure that you participate regularly in your company's revenue forecasting meetings and are sharing your data in a way that builds confidence across your leadership team. This type of collaboration and transparency fosters a data-driven culture and sharpens your team's focus on high-impact activities.

Earlier in the book, I introduced the concept of the REACH Customer Expansion Waterfall. This model outlines a sequence of stages that tracks customers with potential for growth through your expansion pipeline. As you integrate these stages into your workflow, you can apply percentages to each stage that estimate the likelihood that the expansion opportunity will close. This gives you a way to more accurately forecast the expected bookings you will achieve from your expansion pipeline.

Congratulations! If you follow this process, you will feel more confident about your ability to identify, develop, and close expansion opportunities with your existing customers. You will also have a structured process that will impress your CEO, CFO, and Board of Directors and will demonstrate how your team directly drives revenue growth.

REACH
CUSTOMER EXPANSION WATERFALL

CUSTOMERS WITH EXPANSION POTENTIAL
This is a customer who could benefit from purchasing more of your product or service and that fits into your company's definition of a candidate for future expansion.

CUSTOMER SUCCESS QUALIFIED EXPANSION LEAD
CS qualifies expansion leads by scoring them on REACH factors to define the Growth Propensity Index™. CS also nurtures the customer to increase their likelihood and readiness for growth. Specific expansion recommendations are uncovered and identified.

SALES ACCEPTED EXPANSION LEAD
The lead has been formally accepted by the receiving function (AM or AE) which agrees to work the lead according to a timeline. The CSM and AM/AE collaborate to define a joint expansion plan to capitalize on the potential expansion and address any underlying barriers.

SALES QUALIFIED EXPANSION OPPORTUNITY
The expansion lead has been transitioned to an expansion opportunity that has an estimated dollar value and a time frame to close. A joint expansion close plan is developed and followed.

CLOSED/WON EXPANSION BUSINESS
The expansion opportunity is closed.

METRICS THAT MATTER: Imagine how impressed your CEO, CFO, and Board will be when you add structure, rigor, and data-driven activities to the expansion process. You can do this!

Celebrate Your Results

Think for a minute about how differently your executives will look at you and your team after you implement REACH and start seeing results. Today, many Customer Success and Account Management teams struggle to demonstrate their teams' value in achieving company-level outcomes. These teams also often need help demonstrating a connection between their work and the revenue or profitability growth the leadership team needs to see. Their teams are often seen as a cost center.

By implementing REACH, you will be able to demonstrate a structured process that delivers predictable, measurable growth from your existing customer base. This would be a huge achievement to reposition you and your organization in the mind of your CEO and executive team.

Think about what the executive team will see differently.

1. Rigorous structure to identify potential high-growth accounts.

2. Ability to quantify and prioritize accounts with a data-driven approach.

3. Visibility and transparency to the status of and insights about each account.

4. Account Expansion Plans for expanding the relationship with action items and timelines.

5. Pipeline and forecast reports that are believable and are based on data and insights.

6. Expansion Close Plans that provide structure and efficiency to close deals.

7. Outcomes that demonstrate the value your teams are contributing to top-line revenue.

These executives will also see that you feel more confident in your ability to deliver repeatable, predictable expansion growth results that directly contribute to revenue growth. What could be better?

CHAPTER REVIEW

 QUESTIONS TO CONSIDER

- What one step can you take now to apply the REACH Framework™ when working with your customers?
- How would applying REACH's structured framework contribute to your ability to grow revenue from your existing customers more efficiently and predictably?
- What additional skill development, training, or resources are needed to apply REACH? How can you acquire the assistance required? What resources can help you?
- What barriers might you need to overcome to leverage REACH? What teams do you need to work with more closely? How do you start to address those challenges?

 ACTION PLAN

- Discuss the REACH Framework™ with your manager and your team to identify ways the framework can help you accelerate growth from your existing customers.
- Identify the skills, training, and resources your team would need to implement REACH across your business.
- Add the listening and probing techniques from this chapter into your customer interactions to help you identify clues and expansion opportunities.
- Develop expansion account plans for your high-potential customers that incorporate elements of REACH.
- Identify ways to capture each account's status and progress according to REACH. Consider building the REACH Framework™ into your CRM system or Customer Success Platform.

BONUS CHAPTER
How to Overcome Excuses and Start Using REACH

It's common for Customer Success and Account Management teams to encounter mental barriers when they are asked to drive expansion revenue – those nagging doubts and perceived roadblocks that impede progress. In my discussions with hundreds of leaders and frontline team members, these barriers are often excuses. These blocks are deeply engrained ways of thinking about Customer Success Managers' roles and responsibilities that define their comfort zones and limit growth.

But what if these excuses are unfounded fears and misconceptions waiting to be debunked? Or what if you are required to break through these barriers for you to keep your job in the future? In this book, we confront these excuses head-on. We will demonstrate how the REACH Framework™ empowers you to overcome these limitations, adapt your mindset, develop the skills you will need to be impactful now, and stay relevant in the future. Let's talk about a few of the common concerns that I hear.

1. "Suggesting additional products might jeopardize my customer's trust."

Trust is built on honesty and value. If you believe your solution can bring value to your customers, it is your responsibility to share that solution. When you introduce solutions that meet your customer's needs, you deepen that trust. The chapter on Customer Value shows you ways to overcome this concern.

2. "I don't have the right skills or training to handle expansion conversations."

Skill gaps are an opportunity for growth, not a permanent roadblock. This book provides a roadmap for acquiring the necessary skills and confidence to engage in meaningful expansion conversations. REACH also provides a structured framework that helps you deliver repeatable, predictable results.

3. "I fear being too salesy and hurting our relationship."

Being "salesy" is not about pushing products, it's about solving customer problems. REACH enables you to integrate expansion naturally into conversations without coming across as pushy. The framework in this book will shift your perspective from selling to helping, changing the nature of the conversation with your customers.

4. "It is difficult to prioritize which of my customers have growth potential."

Not all customers have equal potential for growth, but there are signs and indicators that can guide you. This book will introduce a structured framework for evaluating a customer's potential for growing with your company in the future. The framework will enable you to identify and prioritize your customers to maximize your expansion efforts effectively.

5. "We are trusted advisors. Our customers don't want us to sell to them."

Advising is a form of selling – you are selling ideas and solutions. Being a trusted advisor doesn't mean avoiding discussions about new solutions. In fact, your role positions you perfectly to align your offerings with customer goals. The REACH Framework™ shows you how being proactive and consultative can naturally lead to expansion without sacrificing trust.

6. "Selling is the sales team's responsibility."

Expansion is a team sport, and every touchpoint with a customer is an opportunity to grow. This book provides examples and stories that demonstrate how to break down silos and integrate cross-functional efforts to drive revenue growth. In addition, there is a growing trend for Customer Success and Account Management teams to have direct accountability for certain aspects of revenue and revenue growth.

7. "I am not incentivized to identify growth opportunities."

Incentives are not just monetary. They're about career progression and making a tangible impact. We will explore how to align personal success with company growth, creating a win-win scenario. Plus, the expectations for your role are likely evolving, so your incentive is to develop and practice these skills so you can keep your job in the future.

8. "I am overwhelmed with my current workload."

Becoming overwhelmed often comes from a lack of focus and prioritization, not from the workload itself. The REACH Framework™ will enable you to focus your time and effort on the highest-impact expansion activities.

Your Next Steps

First and foremost, I am grateful for your commitment to reading this book. Your dedication to embracing the REACH Framework™ and enhancing your Customer Success or Account Management skills is commendable. You now have a structured process to grow your accounts successfully. The Customer Success and Account Management roles continue evolving, so you must also evolve your skills and behavior. I encourage you to act now to start implementing some of the strategies outlined in this book. Your proactive mindset to adopt REACH can start making a difference today.

Second, while the process outlined in the book to use REACH builds a solid foundation, every company has unique challenges and needs. REACH can be tailored to meet the needs of your company. If you or your team would like assistance in developing and implementing REACH for your business, please contact me at rod@hellocco.com to learn more about my advisory, consulting, training, and certification services.

If you are a sales enablement, Customer Success enablement, or revenue operations training expert interested in licensing and using my methodologies and resources in your practice, please contact me at rod@hellocco.com.

Whether you implement these ideas alone or seek my help, I want you to know that YOU can do this. I know you can evolve your skills to meet the changing times. Please let me know about your progress and how this book helps you and your business.

Rod

About the Author

Rod Cherkas is the CEO and founder of HelloCCO, a strategy consulting firm based in San Mateo, California, serving clients worldwide. He is the author of the best-selling book, *The Chief Customer Officer Playbook: 8 Strategies That Will Accelerate Your Career and Win You a Seat at the Executive Table*. He is the leading global advisor to Chief Customer Officers and their post-sale leaders. His vast experience helps CEOs, CCOs, CROs, and their executive teams increase customer retention rates, accelerate time to value, expand revenue faster, and improve financial performance.

Rod has been a customer-facing executive at several of Silicon Valley's most customer-centric companies including Intuit, RingCentral, Marketo, and Gainsight, helping these last three achieve more than $1 billion in IPOs or exits. He is also an operating advisor to CCOs and post-sale executives at the Warburg Pincus portfolio of companies.

A Philadelphia native, Rod completed his bachelor's degree in economics at Duke University and received his MBA at the Stanford Graduate School of Business. Rod and his wife, Corey, live in San Mateo, California and have three children.

You can stay connected with Rod on social media or through email.

- Follow him on LinkedIn: www.linkedin.com/in/rodcherkas/.

- Send him an email: rod@hellocco.com.

- Learn more about his consulting and advisory services at www.rodcherkas.com.

- Keep up with his latest thought leadership by signing up for his newsletter at www.rodcherkas.com.

The Ultimate Guide for CCOs and Aspiring CCOs!

Are you a CCO looking to drive results and excel in your position?

Are you an aspiring CCO looking to develop and master the skills you need to be a successful CCO?

If you answered YES to either of these questions, then Rod Cherkas' *The Chief Customer Officer Playbook* is a must read as this book will enable you to:

- Understand the scope and expectations of a CCO
- Identify the skills you need to acquire along your career path
- Deliver repeatable, predictable results with confidence
- Gain advocates within your company and across your network
- Improve alignment between you and your executive leaders

Get Your Copy Today!
www.RodCherkas.com/books

What Others Are Saying About *The Chief Customer Officer Playbook*

"A must-read for CCOs and anyone aspiring to be a CCO."

— **Mary Poppen,** President at HRIZONS and former CCO at SAP and LinkedIn

"By far the best book of the year."

— **Chris Hicken,** Office of the CEO at Clickup

"Rod's *Playbook* is going to be the future North Star for how CCOs operate."

— **Kellie Capote,** Chief Customer Officer at Gainsight

"Rod has written the playbook to help guide the future generation of Chief Customer Officers on what the role looks like and the path to get there. He offers a perspective that I don't think anybody else has in the industry."

— **Kate Peter,** GVP of Customer Experience Strategy and Scaled CS at Anaplan

"I love LOVE, LOVE this book!"

—**Ashna Patel,** Manager of Customer Success at Ascent Cloud

"The ideas in Rod's book are not just for technology start-ups and scale-ups. They are relevant for any customer-facing leader or executive across all types of industries and company sizes."

— **Nick Mehta,** CEO of Gainsight

"Customer Success Professionals today are so fortunate to have so many resources as they navigate their careers in CS, and this one tops the charts! Stop what you are doing and go snag a copy of this book!"

— **Kristi Faltorusso,** Chief Customer Officer at Client Success

"Rod draws on present-day customer leaders in the SaaS space providing real-life examples to help others. I wish this guide existed when I first started out."

— **Gemma Cipriani-Espineira,** Founder of CS Angels

"Think of Rod's book as a CS executive coach that understands your world, your pains, your insecurities, and your vulnerabilities. All I kept thinking as I read this book was, 'Where was this guidance when I needed it?!'"

—**Samma Hafeez,** VP of Sales and Customer Success COE at Insight Partners

"Whether you're a CCO, aspiring to be one, work in a related field, or are a CEO, this book offers a comprehensive framework for creating a customer-centric organization and strategy. It's a must-read for anyone looking to drive growth and improve customer satisfaction and loyalty."

—**Rachel Rozen,** Founder and CEO of Connection Catalyst

"Thank you for sharing this book with the world, Rod. It was a great read, well-written, and full of insights."

— **Jean Nairon,** Sr. Director of Customer Experience at Dynatrace

"Rod is one of those CS leaders that continues to pioneer the space. To grow CS in a way that makes everyone win. The customer, the individual contributor, the leadership teams, revenue, and the department overall. If you haven't grabbed this book, you're missing out!"

— **Layton Chaney,** Founder of BetterGrowth and Dean of the CCO School at Pavilion

"I finished *The CCO Playbook* by Rod Cherkas in three days. I think this is the fastest I have finished a book in my life. I started reading, and I couldn't stop until I finished!"

— **Erika Villarreal,** Strategic Customer Success Manager at Eptura

"Fast forward to today, and this book has been my constant companion. This past weekend, I found myself going back through pages as I prepared for an upcoming exec offsite."

—**Rachel Orston,** Chief Customer Officer at Instructure

"Rod's book is a must-read for those looking to understand the role of the CCO and what skills and experience you need to accumulate in your career to attain a CCO position."

—**Michael Horsley,** Director of Customer Success at Hyperscience

"Cherkas has written a powerful playbook not only for CCOs but the entire executive team. It's a new game, and the CCO is the customers' advocate."

—**Michael Gospe,** Customer Advisory Board Strategist and Interim CMO, KickStart Alliance

"An amazing resource for CCOs, aspiring post-sale leaders, and CEOs hiring or managing CCOs."

—**Srikrishnan Ganesan,** Co-Founder at Rocketlane

"Now there is a tangible playbook that can help you get to the C-Suite."

— **Nicole Alrubaiy,** VP of Customer Success at Jellyfish

"Rod's book provides a model and structure for how the CCO role can radically enhance the financial performance of his or her company while staying squarely focused on delivering value and delighting customers."

—**Robert Padron,** Chief Growth Officer at Arise Virtual Solutions

"Rod's playbook does a fantastic job. It decodes all the CCO responsibilities and provides tangible suggestions to navigate your career to become a world-class CCO."

—**Angie Holt,** SVP of Customer Success at Datadog

"This is the book that has been missing, not only for aspiring CCOs but to educate the business world about the importance of a CCO. I have not seen a career framework for senior leaders like this before."

—**Jennifer Baca,** Manager of Enterprise Customer Success at Zoom

"This book will help you make your CEO and your CFO look good. It will make your CEO say, 'This person is going someplace and maybe they can be my replacement.'"

—**Omid Razavi,** SVP of Customer Success at Alluxio and Founder of SuccessLab

"This is a fantastic resource that I would classify as required reading for any aspiring leader in the Customer Success or Post-Sale world. I love the specific, actionable recommendations and the many real-life examples from CCOs and CS leaders."

—**Laurence Leong,** VP of Customer Success at Jamf

"Rod's book is the ideal guide for anyone considering a C-level, customer-facing role as his or her next career move. It is an indispensable, practical guide to successfully grow into the role of CCO."

—**Hannah Thompson,** Chief Operating Officer at Avantia Law

"As a recently-promoted CCO, this book really helped me to understand more about my role and how I can provide the most valuable impact to my company. I am sure that Rod's book will help other leaders in the same way. It is a must-read for every Customer Success leader, no matter what role they have."

—**Marko Müller,** Chief Operating Officer at Staffbase

"We don't have a school for how to do Customer Success and Services. There really are few mentors out there. Rod brings that guidance, expertise, and value."

—**Inger Rarick,** former SVP of Customer Success at Sendoso

"I loved this book! It provides a framework for the key attributes of a great CCO and a tactical path on how to get to this level. I felt myself nodding my head as I read through each page."

— **Star Hofer,** Chief Customer Officer at A.K.A. New Media Inc.

"On every page, I felt there was something of special interest to me or useful content. Rod has written a great book!"

— **Paula Sobb,** Chief Customer Officer at iN2L

"*The CCO Playbook* demystifies core concepts and tasks required to grow into the CCO role."

—**Karla Kannan,** Senior Vice President of Customer Experience at BirchStreet

"The writing is clear, concise, and action oriented. Rod has a great book."

—**Christine Rimer,** Chief Customer Officer at Guideline

"I enjoyed the pace and the progressive layout of so many relevant customer experience topics. Rod's voice shines through, making this book interesting and not academic."

— **Mathilde Sanson,** Chief Customer Officer at Black Swan Data

"I would recommend that anyone going up for a promotion read this book."

—**Laura Lakhwara,** former Director of Customer Success at UIPath

"Rod's book was an engaging read. The strategic framework is easy to follow with all the little tips and tricks. It allowed me to reflect on my career path. I found myself creating my own action plan as I read each chapter."

—**Tiffany Taylor,** Senior Director of EDU Success and Education at Handshake

"This book fills a huge gap with detailed, actionable, and proven insights into the emerging CCO role. There is no one better than Rod to have taken on this challenge."

—**Amit Kandpal,** Customer Success Leader at Netskope

"Rod takes decades of knowledge and condenses it into a consumable book so we all can benefit."

—**Mike Lee,** Manager of Customer Success at Avalara

"This book gives you tangible exercises. I also like the real-world examples."

—**Brian Hartley,** Enterprise Customer Success at DX

"Rod has written an effective guide that demystifies the potential paths to CCO. This book provides actionable insights, thought leadership, and a strategic roadmap to get there."

—**Ben Collier,** Director of Professional Services at Freshworks

"Can't recommend Rod Cherkas and his book enough. A must read for anyone navigating his or her career while fighting for a better customer experience."

—**Christina Garnett,** Founder of Pocket CCO and Host of The Woman's MBA podcast

Get Your Copy Today!
www.RodCherkas.com/books

Acknowledgments

To Corey, my wife, thank you for encouragement, support, and kindness as I have embarked on this next exciting phase of my career. Most of all, thank you for being a role model and mother to our kids. I couldn't have written this second book without you.

Thank you to my children Zack, Shelby, and Marlee. You demonstrate an intense curiosity for learning, developing new skills, and doing hard things. That inspired me as I wrote my second book.

To my brothers, Michael and Kevin, and to my Uncle Gary, thank you for your unwavering support for me and my family. You make us feel so loved and connected, even when we live far away.

Thank you to:

Nick Mehta, Dan Steinman, and Jim Eberlin, who helped create a profession and career path for those of us who love to design great customer experiences, deliver company-impacting results, and drive innovation.

My friends and executives at companies including Gainsight, ChurnZero, Totango, Catalyst Software, ClientSuccess, Vitally, Planhat, SmartKarrot, Rocketlane, GuideCX, Certinia, Kantata, and Salesforce, who enable execution and drive innovation for post-sale teams.

Lisa Larter for encouraging me to share my thought leadership through writing and speaking. And thank you for supporting me with expert guidance and advice as I continue to grow my consulting practice.

Cass Bald for partnering with me to hone my messaging, experiment with new channels of communication, and build my professional brand. I always enjoy our collaboration and innovation.

Dave Praetorius for your design expertise and sharp eye for making things visually impactful. Your work on the book cover and my website were phenomenal.

Dan Janal for your expertise and thought-provoking feedback that enabled me to efficiently complete this second book. You make the book-writing process easy and enjoyable.

Weston Lyon, Jenny Butterfield Lyon, and Tracey Miller for the outstanding design, proofreading, and publishing of this book. Your great work turned my ideas into an easy-to-read, beautiful book.

Sharon Holmes for your ability to translate my ideas and words into appealing visuals that enable my audiences to quickly grasp the concepts and frameworks.

The many people who reviewed my manuscript and provided insightful assistance, suggestions, and feedback: Rob Schmeltzer, Maranda Dziekonski, Kristine Kukich, Pam Micznik, Cory Black, Jonathan Romanowsky, Marilyn Lin, Mary Poppen, Laurence Leong, Fiona Gill, Tony Smart, and Jeremy Meyers. Each of you contributed to making this book better for our peers and community.

The incredible thought leaders, executives, and investors who share their expertise, thought-leadership, and stories and whose insight elevates this book: Maranda Dziekonski, Shari Srebnick, Rob Schmeltzer, Kristi Faltorusso, Layton Chaney, Nick Mehta, AJ Gandhi, Gemma Cipriani-Espineira, Mary Poppen, Lynn Tsoflias, Samma Hafeez, Gourab De, Brendan Farnand, Sabrina Leblanc, Kevin Cherkas, Hilary Jules, David Wagonfeld, Roderick Jefferson, Laura Lakhwara, Robbie Baxter, Daphne Costa Lopes, Emilia D'Anzica, Chad Horenfeldt, Alex Turkovic, Erika Villarreal, Donna Weber, Jay Nathan, Josh Schachter, Bhavika Kochhar, Mickey Powell, Kelley Turner, Ryan Weisert, Bryan Fucetola, Tracy Henriques, Carly Bell, Matt French, Adam Young, Felix Higgs, Kristen McKenna, Nathan Jones, Jonathan Schradi, Cory Black, Kody Bradford, Amy Elrod, Jen Schoell, Omid Razavi, Kelly Hook, and Elizabeth Blass.

The hundreds of Chief Customer Officers, Chief Revenue Officers, Customer Success leaders, Account Management leaders, and front-line CSMs and Account Managers I have met who work tirelessly for your customers, your employees, your colleagues, and your shareholders. I see you. I hear you. I appreciate all that you do every day. I love how you drive constant innovation, learn quickly, and share your best practices with others.

A few of the outstanding managers who took a chance on me and brought me into their companies as an employee over the years. I was so lucky to have met you and made a connection in a way that made you confident enough to hire me. I learned so much from you and appreciate that you took a risk on me: Ellen Perelman, David Sipes, Jason Holmes, and Ashvin Vaidyanathan.

Made in the USA
Columbia, SC
24 April 2025